THE CHOSEN

NOTES

including
- *Life and Background of the Author*
- *Introduction to the Novel*
- *Historical Introduction to the Novel*
- *A Brief Synopsis*
- *List of Characters*
- *Critical Commentaries*
- *Character Analyses*
- *Critical Essays*
- *Review Questions and Essay Topics*
- *Selected Bibliography*

by
Stephen J. Greenstein, M.A.

WILEY
Wiley Publishing, Inc.

CliffsNotes™ *The Chosen*

Published by:
Wiley Publishing, Inc.
111 River Street
Hoboken, NJ 07030
www.wiley.com

Copyright © 1999 Wiley Publishing, Inc., Hoboken, New Jersey
ISBN: 978-0-7645-8509-8
Printed in the United States of America
12 11 10 9
MA/TQ/QW/QV/IN

Published by Wiley Publishing, Inc., Hoboken, New Jersey
Published simultaneously in Canada

CONTENTS

THE CHOSEN
Notes

LIFE AND BACKGROUND OF THE AUTHOR

In *The Chosen*, Chaim Potok (pronounced **Hi** em **Poe** talk) describes the condition of American Jews living in two cultures, one secular and one religious. To a great degree, he is describing not only the lives of the characters in the novel but his own life—according to Potok, the novel is very much an autobiography of his young-adult life.

Originally named Herman Harold, Potok was born in New York City on February 17, 1929, to Polish-Jewish immigrants Benjamin Max Potok and Mollie Friedman Potok. His father had emigrated from Poland to the United States in 1921. Prior to the Great Depression, Mr. Potok sold stationery; following the Depression, he became a jeweler. Chaim Potok, along with his younger brother and two younger sisters, was raised in the Orthodox Jewish religion. (His brother eventually became a rabbi, and his sisters both married rabbis.) As with many young boys raised in the Orthodox Jewish religion, he attended Jewish parochial schools, most notably Talmudic Academy of Yeshiva College. (Orthodox Jews believe that Jewish law and practice must be strictly observed. They believe that the Old Testament, known as the Torah—**Tore** ah—and considered to contain the central, most important tenets of the Jewish religion, was given to the Jewish people at Mount Sinai by God and is literally true. It is, they say, eternal, authentic, and binding. No change is permitted.)

Even though he was content growing up within his Jewish religion and culture, Potok sensed that there existed a world beyond his Jewish one that he wanted to experience. As he writes in his essay "Culture Confrontation in Urban America: A Writer's Beginning":

> I had little quarrel with my Jewish world . . . but beyond our apartment, there was an echoing world that I longed to

embrace: it streamed in upon me, its books, movies, music, appealing not only to the mind, but also to the senses.

When Potok was about fifteen years old, he read *Brideshead Revisited*, by English novelist Evelyn Waugh. By his own admission, Potok was impressed. He has commented about the novel, "Evelyn Waugh reached across the chasm that separated my tight New York Jewish world from that of the upper-class British Catholics in his book. I remember finishing the book and marveling at the power of this creativity." Although doing so was frowned upon in his religious training, he read more secular literature, including James Joyce's *A Portrait of the Artist as a Young Man*, which greatly influenced him. Reading novels that challenged his Jewish beliefs, he wondered whether it was possible to be a Jew and an American simultaneously, asking, "Was it possible to live in a religious culture and a secular culture at the same time?"

Potok treasured his Jewish religion and culture but believed that change was necessary and unavoidable. Not surprisingly, he tried to blend American and Jewish ways while he attended New York's Yeshiva University, a Jewish-sponsored school offering both religious and nonreligious courses. He received a B.A., summa cum laude, in English literature from Yeshiva University in 1950.

After his graduation from Yeshiva University, Potok studied for and received ordination as a rabbi in 1954 at the Jewish Theological Seminary of America, a New York institution sponsored by the Conservative branch of Judaism, a less restrictive form of Judaism in terms of religious observances and behaviors. Whereas the Orthodox Jewish movement frowns upon religious change, the Conservative movement suggests that change has always been a feature of Jewish tradition. While studying for rabbinic ordination, Potok also earned a master's degree in Hebrew literature from the Jewish Theological Seminary of America.

Following service as a United States Army chaplain in Korea from 1955 to 1957, Potok married and began a notable teaching and publishing career in Jewish studies. From 1957 to 1959, he was an instructor at the University of Judaism, the Los Angeles campus of the Jewish Theological Seminary of America. He served as scholar-in-residence at Har Zion Temple in Philadelphia (1959-63) and was on the faculty at the Teachers Institute, Jewish Theological

Seminary of America (1963-64). He then served as managing editor of *Conservative Judaism* (1964-65) and editor-in-chief of the Jewish Publication Society (1965-74). He earned a Ph.D. in philosophy at the University of Pennsylvania in 1965. Incidentally, he began writing *The Chosen* while he was still working on his doctoral degree. He would write sections of *The Chosen* during the morning and then focus on his dissertation during the afternoon. Since 1974, he has served as a special projects editor at the Jewish Publication Society.

The Chosen, published in 1967, is Potok's first published novel. Following its publication, Potok continued his investigation into the dilemmas of living simultaneously in a Jewish culture and a secular culture in his novels *The Promise* (1969) and *My Name Is Asher Lev* (1972). In 1975, he published the autobiographical *In the Beginning* and then returned to the theme of Jewish versus secular cultural conflict in *The Book of Lights* (1981), *Davita's Harp* (1985), and *The Gift of Asher Lev* (1990). In 1996, Potok published the non-fiction book *The Gates of November: Chronicles of the Slepak Family*, in which he chronicles a father and son's struggle to understand each other. Throughout his works, Potok returns again and again to such father/son relationships as those in *The Chosen* and *The Gates of November*.

Throughout his distinguished career as a writer and scholar, Potok has received numerous awards. For example, *The Chosen* won the Edward Lewis Wallant Award. Potok's novel *The Promise* received the Anthenaeum Prize, and his novel *The Gift of Asher Lev* was awarded the National Jewish Book Award for Fiction. He received an Honorary Doctorate in Humane Letters in 1997 from La Sierra University. That same year, he was awarded the National Foundation for Jewish Culture's Jewish Cultural Achievement Award for Literature.

INTRODUCTION TO THE NOVEL

Potok's novel *The Chosen* concerns the tensions of living a religious life in a secular society. This conflict is reflected through an examination of two Jewish communities in the Williamsburg area of Brooklyn, New York. Two Jewish boys, an ultra-religious

Hasidic Jew named Danny Saunders and a Modern Orthodox Jew named Reuven (Roo ven) Malter, discuss the realities of trying to be committed, religiously observant Jews in a secular American society. The main theme in the novel is Danny's conflict between his desire for secular knowledge and his obligations to his father, Rabbi Saunders, and his father's followers.

Reuven Malter is the son of Modern Orthodox Jew and teacher David Malter. Even though the elder Malter is religiously observant, he encourages Reuven to explore nonreligious thought. Thus Reuven is thoroughly acquainted with Western secular tradition. But Reuven has conflicts of his own. His father teaches Judaism from a scientific point of view, but the instructor at Hirsch College adheres to a more traditional, religious orientation.

Relationships between fathers and sons are important in *The Chosen*, especially in the choices of the sons' careers. Danny's father expects him to become a rabbi and leader of his Hasidic sect, following the tradition of generations, while Reuven's father lets him choose his own path.

The novel's action begins symbolically with a softball game between the Jewish parochial schools that Danny and Reuven attend. Potok sets up the game to highlight the differences between Danny's branch of Judaism and Reuven's.

During the softball game, a ball hit by Danny strikes Reuven in the eye and puts him in the hospital. Despite the boys' initial antagonism—Reuven blames Danny for deliberately hitting him with the ball—the boys develop a warm friendship. They discuss their feelings about their respective Jewish sects and about their fathers. Over the course of the novel, *The Chosen* focuses on and gradually expands Reuven and Danny's discussions.

Central to the novel are Potok's concerns about Jews who live in the United States. He asks how much a committed, religious Jew can participate in American society without forfeiting a sense of Jewishness, or the perceptions of what it means to be a Jew. Potok also questions how much an American Jew wanting to participate fully in American society can practice Judaism without giving up the sense of being an American. Can a balance be struck between these two apparently diverse concerns?

HISTORICAL INTRODUCTION TO THE NOVEL

Since the seventeenth century, and especially since the nineteenth century, more than 45 million people, representing many ethnic and religious groups, have come to America seeking religious freedom and economic opportunity. Included in this large number of immigrants are Jews. Jews are members of both a religious group and an ethnic group, with ethnic traits and traditions that lie outside their religion. Knowing something about Jewish history can enhance an understanding of *The Chosen*.

Jews first came to America in 1654. At the time of the American Revolutionary War, their number totaled about 2,000. Most earned their living as merchants. Because they had been persecuted as a visible community in Europe, pre-1820 American Jews generally emphasized that they were simply members of a religious faith, not a specific community. Colonial Jews tended to live in major American cities, such as Philadelphia, Charleston, and New York.

Most Jews who came to the United States during the colonial period were Sephardim—descendents of Spanish Jews. (*Sepharad* is the Hebrew word for Spain.) Jews were expelled from Spain in 1492, and Spanish Jews immigrated to Holland, the Ottoman Empire (which included parts of Europe, Asia, and North Africa), and some areas of the Americas in search of refuge. Although the Jewish population in colonial America was small, Jews embraced their new homeland and accommodated themselves into the majority Christian population. By the early nineteenth century, some Sephardic Jews in America had even converted to Christianity.

German Jews. Other Jews who arrived in the United States in the eighteenth and nineteenth centuries came from Central Europe and spread throughout the United States, establishing communities in almost every state. These Jews had suffered persecution in Europe since the First Crusade in the eleventh century and were often forced by government authorities to live in ghettos.

Even though the civil life of Jews in the German states and in Western Europe had improved by 1820, other factors prompted large numbers of German Jews to immigrate to the United States. These included economic downturns and regular eruptions of anti-Semitism (hatred of Jews). Moreover, it was almost impossible for

Jews to exist as small retailers if the peasants with whom they did business were leaving the rural areas for the cities. Also, Jewish population was increasing heavily—the number of Jews tripled during the nineteenth century, and the need for better economic opportunities was urgent.

These Central European Jews often became peddlers or opened retail shops. By the middle of the nineteenth century, at a time when the United States economy was rapidly expanding, Jewish businesses had become important to the country's economic development. Throughout the country, Jewish peddlers brought merchandise to less-populated towns and villages that had no retail stores. In the folklore and history of American Jews, peddling is described as the way in which some immigrants gradually moved into retail businesses. The usual retail store was small, although some Jewish immigrants built great department stores.

In Europe, before coming to the United States, these Jews had experienced a relaxation of the Orthodox tenets of their Jewish faith. Consequently, when they got to the United States, they created communities founded on the principle of reforming Judaism to fit a more secular way of life. The pragmatic character of American society and the demands of small-town frontier life encouraged flexibility, even in religious matters.

Traditional religious practices, including strict adherence to dietary laws and to the rules of the Sabbath and religious holy days, were altered in America. By 1881, the American Jewish population had assimilated into American culture and adapted their religious observances to a more relaxed American life.

The Eastern European Jewish Migration to the United States. In 1881, Russian Czar Alexander II was assassinated. The Russian government blamed Jews for the assassination and undertook violent physical attacks—called pograms—on them. In 1882, the government passed the May Laws, which sharply curtailed Jews' ability to earn a living and participate in Russian society.

Faced with outright hostility and ostracism, many Jews left Eastern Europe, believing that the United States offered religious tolerance, economic opportunity, and the possibility for starting a new life. Eastern European Jews referred to the United States as the "goldineh medinah," Yiddish for *golden land*. In spite of physical problems leaving Eastern Europe—the difficulty of getting a passport, the high price of a steamship ticket, and the hunger, thirst, and sickness caused by the sea passage itself—about two and a half million Eastern European Jews came to the United States between 1881 and 1914.

Almost all Eastern European Jewish immigrants after 1870 stopped in New York City. A great number of them stayed there and found their way to a section of New York called the Lower East Side, a twenty-square-block area south of Houston Street and east of the Bowery. By 1910, about 542,000 Jews lived in this area, and overcrowding became a growing concern. The streets were crowded, but the tiny apartments in which the immigrants lived were often worse. One immigrant remembers sharing two rooms with two parents and five other boarders—people taken in to help pay the rent. As Gerald Sorin recounts in his book *A Time for Building: The Third Migration,* "The cantor rehearses, a train passes, the shoemaker bangs, ten brats run around like goats, and at night we all try to get some sleep in the stifling roach-infested two rooms."

At this time, the garment industry was experiencing great growth in the United States, with New York City as its center. By 1897, about 60 percent of the New York City Jewish labor force was employed in the apparel industry. By 1910, the city produced 70 percent of the nation's women's clothing and 40 percent of its men's clothing, creating jobs for newly arriving Jews.

On the religious front, the majority of Jews who came to the United States from Europe between 1881 to 1914 were Orthodox Jews. Orthodox Jews believe that the Torah is the basis for the structure of religious law that applies to all areas of a Jew's life.

In addition to the written Torah, Orthodox Jews adhere to an oral tradition that they believe was communicated directly from God to Moses, who then transferred it to the religious leadership of the Jewish people. This oral tradition was finally written down in the second century A.D. and is called the Talmud (**Tall** mood). The Talmud explains and clarifies the frequently controversial laws expressed in the Torah.

For Orthodox Jews, Jewish law applies to all parts of life—for example, when and how to pray and which blessings to say at a wide variety of daily activities. But Orthodox Jews had a difficult time fulfilling their religious obligations while living in the United

States, an overwhelmingly secular society. Business life was regulated by a Christian calendar, and many Orthodox Jews, wanting to improve their lives economically, encountered conflicts between religious observances and economic necessities that they had to resolve in favor of American demands.

For example, Saturday is the Jewish Sabbath, a day of rest, but it is an ordinary workday in American culture. Moreover, it is difficult for a business person to pray three times a day and remain faithful to Jewish dietary laws and other Jewish principles. A noted Jewish professional of the time, Rabbi Mordecai Kaplan, once remarked that "the economic factor makes even the distinctive religious expression of Jewish life, particularly Sabbath observance, very difficult."

To resolve this religious versus economic conflict, many Orthodox Jews believed that, in order to ensure that their children were not completely secularized, they would have to make some changes in their daily lives. They saw their children, raised in the United States, wandering away from Jewish practice and observance, ashamed of their parents with their foreign accents and clothing, their tastes for European foods and styles of life, and their old-fashioned customs and religion. Moreover, because the parents were uneducated in American ways, their children saw them as members of an ignorant, lower-class ethnic world. This conflict was aggravated by government efforts and social demands on immigrant groups to adjust to American culture.

So the elder Jews established for their offspring the Young Israel movement, which began on the Lower East Side in 1912 with a mission to help young Jews feel completely American while remaining faithful to Judaism. Young Israel built a microcosm of the larger American society. Through the years, it developed Boy Scout troops, athletic leagues, and sisterhoods, and it established an employment service to assist Sabbath-observing Jews find employment when discrimination against Jews in employment was legal and widespread.

Modern Orthodox Jews. The Young Israel movement was one of the foundations of the Modern Orthodox movement in the United States during the 1920s, 1930s, and 1940s. Its various positions on such things as spiritual and secular matters are embraced by David and Reuven Malter in Potok's *The Chosen*.

Modern Orthodox Jews believe that they can be committed to time-honored Jewish traditions and observances and yet still participate in the general American society. For example, they dress like other Americans while still adhering to Orthodox law. They are committed to "Torah Judaism and secular learning," the motto of New York's Yeshiva University, which Modern Orthodox Jews founded. They see their Orthodox position not in terms of narrow Orthodox restrictions but in terms of the larger issues of the Jewish and general societies.

Modern Orthodox Jews are traditional in their reliance upon the wisdom of the past and their view of tradition as an anchor, or foundation, in their lives. But because they believe in the benefits to be had from interacting with the modern world, they remain attached to modern society. Samuel Heilman, a prominent Modern Orthodox Jew, commented on this dual commitment in Natalie Gittelson's "American Jews Rediscover Orthodoxy," *The New York Times Magazine*, September 30, 1984:

> I live in two worlds. I have thought at times of abandoning one of these worlds in favor of the other. But I realize that for me there can be no such flight. Each world has become more attractive by the possibility of life in the other. So, like many Orthodox Jews . . . I have tried wherever possible to remove the boundaries between the two worlds and find a way to make myself a whole person.

Hasidic Jews. Other Orthodox Jews do not want to change their ways of living to assimilate completely into an exclusively American culture. These Jews are represented in *The Chosen* in the characters of Danny Saunders and his father, Reb Saunders. They are Hasidic (Hah see dick) Jews, and their movement is called Hasidism. The word *Hasidic,* of Hebrew origin, means *pious one*.

The Hasidic movement dates from the eighteenth century, when a traveling healer and storyteller named Israel ben Eliezer began to preach in Eastern Europe to the common Jewish people. Preaching a Judaism that relied less on books and more on personal experiences, he perceived that Jewish practices of the day, with their overemphasis on fine scholarly issues and complicated ways of studying Jewish texts, were alienating the common Jew.

Given the name Ba'al Shem Tov, which means *Master of the Good Name*, he began to preach that God accepts prayer not only through scholarship and study but also through piety, love, prayer, and worship full of song and dance. He emphasized the mystical presence of God in everything. It was very important, he said, to be cheerful. Serving God cannot be done in an atmosphere of gloom. A Jew who is conscious of God's closeness is automatically happy.

In addition, the Ba'al Shem Tov decreed that excessive fasting and self-denial are worthless goals. It is far better to enjoy God's blessings and be grateful for them. One should not deny material possessions. "The smoke of my pipe," the Ba'al Shem Tov said, "can be an offering of incense to God."

The Ba'al Shem Tov expressed himself by using simple sayings and stories that the people listening to him could understand. As examples of his principles, he used the life around him. One such saying is, "Get rid of your anger by doing a favor for the one with whom you are angry." Another wise saying of his is, "Bear in mind that life is short, and that with every passing day you are nearer to the end. . . . Do not waste your time with meaningless quarrels with people."

The Ba'al Shem Tov traveled throughout Eastern Europe, and his reputation spread quickly. Gradually, large numbers of Jews started to depart from their towns to follow him and his disciples. These many followers eventually became the leaders of the Hasidic movement.

Not surprisingly, opposition to the Ba'al Shem Tov's teachings grew. The most important criticism of the Hasidic way of life was that it de-emphasized Jewish learning and scholarship. Those who believed that Hasidism was a threat to Jewish life and culture were called Mitnagdim (Meet **nog** dim). They especially criticized the Hasidic belief in the position of the tzaddik (**sah** dick), also called Rebbe (**Reb** eh), short for rabbi—the Ba'al Shem Tov's position within the movement—and the apparent Hasidic belief that he could issue divine blessings independent of the Torah.

Many non-Hasidic Jews criticize the belief in the position of a tzaddik because they perceive that giving a tzaddik such an exalted position comes too close to idol worship, which is condemned in Jewish practice. Jews, they suggest, attempt to draw near to God directly and require no middle person to act as a conveyor of God's word. They concede that a rabbi is someone who knows more about Jewish law and practice than a layperson, but a rabbi is not needed in many instances—for example, all that is required to hold a prayer service is the presence of ten Jewish males. Indeed, a Jewish saying states: "Nine rabbis do not make a religious service, but ten cobblers do." The central position that the Hasidim give to their tzaddik is not shared by most non-Hasidic Jews.

The Hasidim firmly believe that their manner of approaching God is the correct one and that all other ways are wrong. Furthermore, they believe that their own rebbe, or tzaddik, is the authority on Jewish religious matters. Each rebbe has distinct ways of looking at Jewish religious practice, but each sect believes that its own rebbe is absolutely right. Moreover, the Hasidim believe that there are great differences between Hasidic and Modern Orthodox beliefs. The differences between these beliefs serve as a backdrop to Potok's *The Chosen*.

Whereas many Orthodox and non-Orthodox Jews seek to integrate themselves into American society, the Hasidim keep themselves greatly isolated from American culture and influence, trying to re-create a more traditional, European-style society. They reject any attempts of assimilation into the secular world and fight any form of change within their culture.

A BRIEF SYNOPSIS

The Chosen begins in 1944 with a softball game in a Jewish section of Brooklyn, New York, between students from two Jewish parochial schools. Each team represents a different Jewish sect with a different level of religious observance. Danny Saunders represents a Hasidic sect led by his father, Reb (short for rabbi) Saunders. Reuven Malter leads the opposing team, which is composed of Modern Orthodox Jews, who are not as ultra-Orthodox in terms of their religious observances as Hasidic Jews are. Reuven is the son of David Malter, a yeshiva professor.

During the game, Danny hits a ball that strikes Reuven in the face, injuring his eye and sending him to the hospital for surgery. Danny visits Reuven in the hospital and apologizes for hitting him with the ball. At first, Reuven rejects Danny's apology, but at the urging of his father, he becomes Danny's friend. Speaking of himself, Danny tells Reuven that he will inherit his father's position, as is common in the Hasidic tradition, and become a rabbi, but he also admits that he would rather become a psychologist. Reuven learns that Danny has been raised in virtual silence—the only time Reb Saunders talks to his son is when they study Talmud together.

Danny confesses that studying only the Talmud is boring and that he secretly reads secular books in the public library. According to Danny, even though Jews have an obligation to obey God, sometimes he is not sure what God wants. Reuven wants to become a rabbi but also has a strong interest in math. Danny makes the perceptive and rather amusing observation that he *has* to be a rabbi but doesn't want to be one, and Reuven does not have to be a rabbi but *wants* to be one.

Reuven visits Danny at his home several times and discusses the Torah and other writings with Reb Saunders and Danny. During one of these visits, Reb Saunders talks to Reuven privately. The Reb says that he knows that Danny has been visiting the public library and wants to know what he has been reading. Reuven tells Reb Saunders everything—how Danny met Mr. Malter in the library and how his father helped Danny select reading material. The Reb says that Danny is so brilliant that he cannot talk to him, but he also says with deep emotion that Danny is his most precious possession.

When Mr. Malter suffers a heart attack, Reb Saunders invites Reuven to stay with him and his family until Mr. Malter's health improves. Danny and Reuven spend much time together discussing various literary and Jewish subjects. When they visit Reuven's father in the hospital, Mr. Malter talks passionately about the 6 million Jews slaughtered by Hitler and the Nazis and how the American Jews must help rebuild this human loss. He also supports establishing a Jewish state in Palestine. Jews cannot wait for the Messiah to come to aid them, he argues. They must help themselves. Mr. Malter's position on Palestine contrasts that of Reb Saunders, who says that Palestine cannot become a Jewish state until the Messiah comes.

Danny and Reuven enter Hirsch College for the fall term. Danny is upset that the college psychology department discredits the work of Sigmund Freud, preferring instead the discipline of experimental psychology.

Mr. Malter gives a speech at Madison Square Garden in New York City, urging an end to British control of Palestine and the creation of a Jewish state in its place. Reuven is moved by the speech, but Reb Saunders is furious. He forbids Danny to associate with Reuven. Reuven tells his father about this, adding that it wasn't unexpected. Reuven says to his father that Reb Saunders is a fanatic. Mr. Malter agrees but adds that the fanaticism of people like Reb Saunders has kept the Jewish people alive for the last 2,000 years.

For the rest of the semester, Danny and Reuven do not speak to one another. Reuven finds the estrangement terrible to endure—his grades suffer, and he constantly wonders what Danny is thinking and how he's getting along.

The conflict between Reb Saunders and Mr. Malter continues. Reb Saunders organizes his followers into a group called the League for a Religious Israel. Mr. Malter continues speaking on behalf of a Jewish state in Palestine.

On November 29, 1947, the United Nations decides to partition Palestine into an Arab state and a Jewish state. Reb Saunders condemns the United Nations' announcement and orders Jews to ignore it. The state of Israel is formally proclaimed on May 14, 1948. After the United Nation's action, Reb Saunders' anti-Zionist stance fades in importance as far as the students at Hirsch College are concerned. Danny is again permitted to speak to Reuven, and their rift is healed.

At his professor's suggestion, Danny decides to pursue a Ph.D. in clinical psychology, which means that he will have to renounce his claim to his father's rabbinical position. Danny and Reuven discuss how Danny should tell his father, and Danny also gets advice from Mr. Malter. Ironically, Reb Saunders already knows of Danny's decision.

Through Danny, Reb Saunders invites Reuven to his home for the Passover holiday, and the two young men talk together with Reb Saunders. The Reb recognizes that the boys have become men. Reuven tells the Reb that he is going to become a rabbi. Reb Saunders acknowledges that Danny has chosen a different path; Danny has a brilliant mind and cannot be satisfied within the confines of a Hasidic environment. The Reb trusts that Danny will become a tzaddik for the world in his practice of psychology.

Danny and Reuven graduate from Hirsch College. When Danny comes to say good-bye to Reuven and Mr. Malter before leaving for graduate school at Columbia University, Reuven notices that Danny has shaved his beard and cut off his earlocks, two symbols of the Hasidic faith. Mr. Malter says that Columbia University is not so far away, so Danny should visit them often. The novel ends as Danny agrees to visit the Malters and then leaves.

LIST OF CHARACTERS

Danny Saunders

One of the main characters of the novel, along with Reuven Saunders. Danny, a Hasidic Jew, struggles to combine his father's strict religious practice with his own more secular interest in human psychology.

Rabbi Isaac (Reb) Saunders

Danny's father, and the leader of his Hasidic sect. Reb Saunders personifies the Hasidic "rebbe" (from "rabbi," or teacher) in that he is strict and serious and obeys Jewish law to the letter.

Reuven Malter

Danny's friend and the narrator of the novel. Like Danny, Reuven is an Orthodox Jew. But unlike Danny, Reuven can enter the secular world while still retaining his Orthodox Jewish identity because he is a Modern Orthodox Jew rather than a Hasidic Jew.

David Malter

Reuven's father, who teaches Jewish studies at a yeshiva.

Manya

The Malters' Russian housekeeper.

Mr. Galanter

Reuven's softball coach.

Davey Cantor

The boy on Reuven's softball team who warns Reuven that Danny's yeshiva team members are "murderers."

Tony Savo

A patient who shares Reuven's hospital room. Mr. Savo apparently is a washed-up professional boxer.

Billy Merrit

A young boy who, along with Mr. Savo, shares Reuven's hospital room. Billy is completely blind, which greatly upsets Reuven and Reuven's father because they fear that Reuven could end up the same way if his wounded eye doesn't heal properly.

Roger Merrit

Billy's father, a caring man who dotes on his son.

Dr. Snydman

The doctor who successfully operates on Reuven's damaged left eye.

Mrs. Carpenter

The nurse who cares for Reuven, Mr. Savo, and Billy in the hospital.

Rav Gershenson

Professor of Talmudic study at Samson Raphael Hirsch Seminary and College. Danny and Reuven study the Talmud with him. Although Reuven comes intellectually alive in his classroom, Rav Gershenson asks him not to use his father's—Mr. Malter's—methods of explaining the Talmud in his classroom.

Professor Appleman

Danny's psychology professor at Hirsch College. Appleman specializes in experimental psychology, a field of study that Danny initially dislikes but later accepts as valid, and convinces Danny to pursue an advanced degree in clinical psychology.

Levi Saunders

Danny's sickly younger brother.

CRITICAL COMMENTARIES

BOOK ONE

CHAPTER 1

Summary

On a hot June afternoon in 1944, in Brooklyn, softball teams from two Orthodox Jewish parochial schools play against each other. The two teams have a rivalry based on their different religious beliefs.

Reuven (**Roo** ven) Malter, a Modern Orthodox Jew, narrates the story. His team, with their coach, Mr. Galanter, gets to the softball diamond first and practices while Mr. Galanter encourages them. Their opponents, a team of Hasidic (Hah **see** dick) Jews, arrive. Their coach insists that his team get five minutes of practice time, then he proceeds to sit on the bench and ignore the players while he reads a religious book in Yiddish.

Reuven reminds himself that his father, a Modern Orthodox scholar and teacher at a yeshiva, doesn't mind the differing beliefs of Hasidic Jews but does object to their self-righteousness and their belief that their congregation's leader, or tzaddik (**sah** dick), is the only arbiter of Jewish law. One such tzaddik is Reb Saunders, whose son, Danny, plays on the opposing team.

During the early, hard-fought innings, the Hasidic team is carried by the ability and determination of their leader, Danny. Danny has a way of hitting the ball very hard, right at the pitcher, whom he barely misses on his first hit. The next time Danny's team comes to bat, Reuven is the pitcher. Danny smashes a ball that hits Reuven in the eye, shattering his eyeglasses and causing him great pain. After the game ends, Reuven is rushed to the hospital.

Commentary

Potok opens *The Chosen* by describing the setting and cultural background in which the novel takes place—an area in New York City called Williamsburg, which is heavily populated by Jews. Ironically, the streets of Williamsburg are not paved with gold, as alluded to in the mythical image of America; rather, they're paved with asphalt riddled with potholes. Even the sidewalks are "cracked squares of cement." This description reveals something about the social realities of many immigrant Jews, who came to America seeking economic opportunity but often struggled to make ends meet in their new country.

Culturally, the Jews are divided between ultra-Orthodox Hasidic Jews and Modern Orthodox Jews. For example, although all male Orthodox children attend yeshivas, some yeshivas (including Reuven Malter's) teach more English subjects than other yeshivas do (including Danny Saunders'). Language also separates the different Orthodox Jews: Reuven learns about Jewish subjects in Hebrew; Danny learns these subjects in Yiddish. By mentioning this language difference, Potok introduces the importance that language—or, in Danny's case, silence—plays in the novel.

Danny Saunders and Reuven Malter represent these two Orthodox Jewish sects: Hasidic Jews and Modern Orthodox Jews, respectively. Potok establishes the boys' religious rivalry by having each as the leader of his softball team. Interestingly, no matter what their religious differences, they can find common ground in the very American game of softball. Note that the boys' yeshivas introduced softball to the students as a way to demonstrate American patriotism: World War II is underway at the beginning of the novel. Reuven narrates the newfound importance placed on appearing American: "[T]o be counted a loyal American had become increasingly important to us these last years of the war."

In bringing Danny and Reuven before us, Potok sets the stage for their later religious and secular dialogues, in which the boys oftentimes differ over issues. Their different outlooks on life are symbolized in their manner of dress. Because Reuven and Danny are Orthodox Jews, they wear small, black skullcaps. However, the skullcap is the only outward similarity between their garments. All the boys on Danny's team wear the same outfits; Reuven and his team members have no set uniform.

In addition to their personal rivalry, Reuven and Danny represent their respective fathers, David Malter and Rabbi Isaac Saunders, who is introduced later in the novel, and their fathers' differing religious views. Reuven tells us that his father "had no love at all for Hasidic communities and their rabbinic overlords," of which Danny's father is one. Danny, speaking to Reuven at second base, asks, "Your father is David Malter, the one who writes articles on the Talmud?" When Reuven confirms that David Malter is his father, Danny promises that his team will "kill you apikorsim," a word originally used to describe a Jew who denied basic tenets of Judaism. That Reuven is struck by a ball off Danny's bat at the end of Chapter 1 is symbolic of their—and their fathers'—ideological battles.

Although *The Chosen* focuses on Danny Saunders' struggle to stand up to his father and renounce the leadership position that tradition dictates Danny inherit, Chapter 1 establishes Reuven's own personal struggle to accept Danny and the Hasidic religion that Danny and his father represent. Although Reuven would like to believe that he is more open-minded than Danny, he admits that he has never before had "personal contact" with members of Danny's religious sect. However, he has accepted his own father's critical views concerning Rabbi Saunders' "fanatic sense of righteousness." Reuven, like Danny, must first learn to think for himself and then form his own opinions rather than blindly accepting someone else's. His father, Danny, and Danny's father will help Reuven accomplish this growth.

(Here and in the following sections, difficult words and phrases are explained.)

◦ **Hasidic Jews** (Hah see dick) descendants of Jews who founded the Jewish sect of Hasidism (**Hah** see dism) in eighteenth-century Europe. Hasidism suggests that it is possible to reach a close relationship with God through song and joy rather than only through more formal avenues of prayer. This philosophy of Hasidism was expounded by its leader and founder, Israel Ba'al Shem Tov (Master of the Good Name). In the novel, Hasidic philosophy is represented by Danny Saunders and his father, Rabbi (Reb) Saunders.

- **samovar** an urn with a spigot used for heating water for tea; originated in Russia.

- **Shabbat** another word for the Sabbath, the seventh day of the week reserved for rest and worship; for Jews, the Sabbath is on Saturday.

- **Yiddish** The language of Eastern European Jews, Yiddish comes from German and Polish roots. Hasidic Jews prefer to use Yiddish as an everyday language, believing that the use of Hebrew, the original language of the Jewish people, is a holy tongue; to use Hebrew in an ordinary classroom would desecrate God's name. Reuven's Modern Orthodox sect, however, uses Hebrew in its classrooms.

- **brownstones** residential buildings made of reddish-brown sandstone, common in urban areas.

- **Spanish Civil War** Starting as a military insurrection, this war lasted from 1936 until 1939, involved Italy and Germany on the side of the fascist insurrectionists, and brought General Francisco Franco to power.

- **skullcap** a close-fitting, brimless cap worn by Orthodox Jewish men.

- **earlocks** hair grown long at the temples. Ultra-Orthodox Jewish men obey the Torah precept that directs, "You shall not clip your hair at the temples or mar the edges of your beard. You shall not lacerate your bodies for the dead or tattoo any marks upon yourselves" (Leviticus 19:27-28).

- **yeshiva** (yuh **sheev** ah) a school to which Orthodox Jews send their male children. Half of the academic day is spent on Jewish subjects, and the other half on secular subjects. In the novel, Reuven attends a yeshiva that offers more secular classes than Danny's yeshiva does. At times, this difference causes resentment in Danny, who thinks that Reuven is less observant of Jewish law.

- **Talmud** (Tall mood) the oral law of Judaism, based on rabbis' interpretations of ambiguous laws in the Torah and on issues concerning a wide variety of topics in Jewish life. The oral law was written down in the first century A.D.

- **gentile** a non-Jew.

- **infield** the baseball team members playing the shortstop and first, second, and third base positions.

- **assimilationist**   a person who believes in the inclusion of different racial and ethnic groups into mainstream culture.

- **Semitic**   Jewish.

- **tzizit (tsee** seet)   fringes that hang down from the Jewish prayer shawl and are intended to remind Jews of the necessity of observing Jewish law. The Torah states, "When you look upon it [tzizit], you will remember to do all the commands of the Lord" (Numbers 37:39). Ultra-Orthodox Jewish men, such as the Hasidim, wear a prayer shawl under their clothes and leave the fringes visible over the waists of their trousers.

- **side-curls**   another term for earlocks, defined above.

- **momzer**   (**mom** zer) a colloquial word of derision.

- **apikorsim**   (ah **pik** or sim) a word of disfavor used by the ultra-Orthodox to refer to the Modern Orthodox.

- **Mincha Service**   an afternoon Jewish religious service.

- **shamashim**   (plural of shamash) assistants at a Jewish religious service who perform a variety of functions.

- **shlepper**   a Yiddish word for a person who moves slowly or awkwardly.

- **Hasid**   a Hasidic Jew.

CHAPTERS 2-4

Summary

Mr. Galanter, the coach of Reuven's softball team, takes Reuven to Brooklyn Memorial Hospital, where Reuven has surgery to remove glass from his left eye. The next morning, Reuven introduces himself to the man in the bed on his left, Mr. Savo, a boxer, and the youngster in the bed on his right, Billy, who was blinded in a car accident.

Reuven's father, Mr. Malter, visits Reuven in the hospital and tells him that he will recover completely from the accident. He also says that Danny's father, Reb Saunders, has called him to ask about Reuven's condition. According to Reb Saunders, Danny is very upset about the accident. But Reuven believes that Danny deliberately set out to hit him. Reuven's father disagrees with his son's analysis of the situation and asks him not to speak this way about Danny.

Reuven goes to sleep. When he wakes up, Danny Saunders is standing at his bedside. Danny tells Reuven that he is truly sorry about the accident, but Reuven verbally attacks him. Danny tries to convince Reuven that he is sorry, but to no avail. Finally, he leaves.

When Danny returns the next day, Reuven is surprised at himself because he is happy to see Danny. The boys talk and begin to accept each other, discussing their career aspirations. Danny says that he will become a rabbi and succeed his father as leader of his group of Orthodox Hasidim in the accepted way—the son becomes tzaddik after the father. If he weren't required to become the tzaddik for his sect, Danny would become a psychologist. Reuven says that he may become a rabbi, but his father would like him to become a mathematician.

The next day, Danny tells Reuven about the books he reads unbeknownst to his father, who is very strict about what Danny reads. Danny reads so much because he gets bored studying only Talmud. He says that he met a man at the library who has been advising him on what to read (Danny later learns that the man is Mr. Malter, Reuven's father). Reuven observes that Danny looks like a Hasid but doesn't talk like one. Danny admits that, because of his secular interests, he is in a difficult position, but he also says that somehow he will work out the situation. Yet to Reuven, he seems sad.

Friday comes, and the doctor removes the bandage from Reuven's left eye and finds that his eye seems to be healing properly. Mr. Malter and Reuven leave the hospital.

Commentary

In Chapter 2, Potok introduces us to the two patients who share Reuven's hospital room: Tony Savo and Billy Merrit. Tony Savo, in his middle thirties, is a professional boxer who is in the hospital because of an injury to his right eye. A rather brash but happy-go-lucky man who likes joking with the nurses, he befriends Reuven; Reuven, however, has trouble understanding Mr. Savo and sometimes just nods in response to whatever he says. Billy, whom Reuven guesses is ten or eleven years old, plays a more important role in this chapter. Billy is blind, which greatly upsets Reuven, for Reuven begins to realize just how lucky he is—he is likely to regain sight in his left eye; Billy will not. Billy's blindness also affects Reuven's father, David Malter. When Mr. Malter looks at Billy and Billy's father talking and realizes that Billy is blind, he is momentarily stunned. Reuven notes of his father's watching Billy and Billy's father, "He looked at them a long time. Then he turned back to me. I saw from his face that he knew Billy was blind." Billy's blindness seems to draw Reuven and his father closer together. They appreciate each other's presence.

Reuven is confused when his father tells him that Danny's father, Reb Saunders, has called him twice, asking about Reuven's health. Reuven cannot believe that Reb Saunders would care about him, for he characterizes Reb Saunders like Danny: mean, haughty, and thoroughly detestable. Earlier in Chapter 2, Reuven thinks of how much he hates Danny and therefore hates Danny's father. Of Danny, Reuven thinks, "That Danny Saunders was a smart one, and I hated him. . . . That miserable Hasid!" He perceives—selfishly and incorrectly—that Danny and his father *must* be alike; therefore, if he hates Danny, he must also hate Danny's father. Mr. Malter wants to correct his son's misperceptions but stops himself from doing so. Reuven must learn on his own.

The hatred that Reuven feels for Danny blinds him to any good qualities that Danny possesses. He cannot believe that Danny is sorry for hurting him, even when Mr. Malter tells him that Danny is. At the end of Chapter 2, note that Reuven cannot comprehend what it would be like to be blind. He thinks to himself, "I couldn't imagine what it was like to know that no matter whether my eyes were opened or closed it made no difference, everything was still dark." Ironically, however, at this point in the novel Reuven is metaphorically blind: He cannot accept the possibility that Danny might feel truly sorry for hitting him in the eye with the ball.

David Malter's bringing a radio to Reuven's hospital room so that Reuven can listen to how the war is progressing is an example of Mr. Malter's belief that Jews should not shut themselves off to the outside, more secular world. He says to Reuven, "You should not forget there is a world outside." His statement contrasts our perception of Reb Saunders, who, according to Mr. Malter, is concerned only with religious life.

Chapter 3 begins apparently on D-Day, June 6, 1944, when Allied forces landed at Normandy, France, and began the military operation designed to force Nazi troops stationed in France into submission. Note that Reuven, while listening to the war news on the radio, initially gets out his prayer book, remembers that he is not allowed to read because of the strain on his eye, and prays instead. Reuven does not reject a secular life—represented by the war news—for a completely religious life, but neither does he choose an exclusively secular life over religion; he balances both secular *and* religious worlds, as does his father. In the opening scene of Chapter 3, we also learn that Reuven's father wants Reuven to become a mathematician. Reuven, however, is unsure about this career choice, for he toys with the idea of becoming a rabbi.

Danny's first visit to the hospital to see Reuven is disastrous. Reuven simply cannot accept that Danny would be truly sorry for hitting him in the eye with the ball. No matter how profusely Danny apologizes, Reuven refuses to believe Danny's sincerity and mocks his repentant visitor: "How does it feel to know you've made someone blind in one eye?" When Reuven notices the sad tone of Danny's apologies, he resorts to anger rather than try to understand the sadness in Danny's voice. Intentionally, it seems, Reuven will not accept Danny's attempts at reconciliation. However, Reuven is chastised by his father for not listening to Danny. Mr. Malter explains to his son that the Talmud directs, "If a person comes to apologize for having hurt you, you must listen and forgive him." Reuven's anger has blinded him to the Talmud's teachings. Selfishly, although understandably, he does not recognize that perhaps Danny *needs* Reuven's forgiveness and is extending a hand of friendship. Mr. Malter understands Danny's motivations; Reuven does not.

Having listened to his father's words about forgiveness, Reuven is more responsive to Danny the second time that Danny visits him in the hospital. Reuven is even surprised at how happy he is to see Danny. That the two boys freely express themselves and at least tentatively accept each other's apologies demonstrates a newfound level of maturity in both of them. They are on the way to becoming mature adults. For Danny, although he cannot yet understand why he wanted to hurt Reuven physically during the ballgame, he at least begins questioning his motives.

Reuven and Danny's discussion about Danny's photographic memory leads to Danny's revealing that he does not want to inherit his father's rabbinic position within the Hasidic community. The situation is ironic in that Danny does not want to be a rabbi but is expected to become one; Reuven, on the other hand, does not want to become a mathematician, as his father wants him to, but wants to become a rabbi. The two boys' perceptions of each other are actually *mis*perceptions. For example, when Reuven learns that Danny is considering becoming a psychologist, he humorously thinks to himself, "Danny Saunders, in his Hasidic clothes, seemed to me to be about the last person in the world who would qualify as an analyst." Reuven unfairly compartmentalizes Danny not as an individual person but as only a Hasidic Jew.

Danny's comments about his father at the end of Chapter 3 reveal the silent family life in which he has grown up and recall Book One's epigraph, from Proverbs, and especially the line, "Let your heart hold fast my words." Here at the end of Chapter 3, Danny notes of his father, "He says that words distort what a person really feels in his heart," and that his father, puzzlingly, "wishes everyone could talk in silence." This theme of silence as a language is explored throughout the novel. Danny apparently contemplates for quite a while Reuven's statement that Reb Saunders must be "quite a man," as though Danny is deciding if his father indeed is all that Reuven perceives him to be. However, Danny's silence suggests that he has serious doubts about Reb Saunders, both as a person and as a father.

Reuven's father's visit to the hospital at the beginning of Chapter 4 affords Potok the opportunity to develop David Malter's character. Pragmatic yet sensitive to his son's needs, Mr. Malter advises his son to accept Danny as his friend. His insistence that Reuven and Danny become friends emphasizes the reciprocal needs of each boy to make the other boy a confidant. Mr. Malter apparently knows more about Danny and his needs than he lets on to his son. During his visit, note that his philosophy of life is very practical and open-minded. For example, when Reuven says that he wishes he were outside rather than cooped up in the hospital,

Mr. Malter responds, "No one knows he is fortunate until he becomes unfortunate. . . . That is the way the world is." Here, we are reminded of when, in Chapter 2, Mr. Malter first realized that Billy, one of Reuven's roommates, is blind: He appreciates even more his son's eyesight and well-being, which is inferred in the emotions that he experienced and stifled: "His voice was husky, and it trembled." Later in Chapter 4, after listening to Reuven relate his conversation with Danny, Mr. Malter says, "People are not always what they seem to be. . . . That is the way the world is, Reuven." His repeated sentence, "That is the way the world is," demonstrates his pragmatism.

When Danny next visits Reuven in the hospital, Danny is much more open with his feelings and doubts than he was previously. The two boys even find a commonality between them: They were born in the same hospital. Much more important than their brief discussion about where they were born is Danny's doubts about his place in the world. Staring out the hospital room's window at people below, Danny says to Reuven, "They look like ants. Sometimes I get the feeling that's all we are—ants." And after once again explaining that his father never talks to him except about religion, he wonders aloud, "Sometimes I'm not sure I know what God wants." Danny questions his own worth in terms of religion and the secular world. He is at the point in life at which he's trying to discover what he wants out of life and what his place in the world is. To help him in this discovery, he has begun reading nonreligious texts, including fiction and works about evolution, secular reading that Reb Saunders certainly would not approve—if he knew.

The contrasts between the boys are outlined further in Chapter 4. For example, Danny, obviously more at ease around Reuven, comments how he is expected to become a rabbi but doesn't want to; Reuven, on the other hand, doesn't have to become a rabbi but wants to. When Reuven says that he's studying mathematics, and especially mathematical logic, or symbolic logic, Danny admits that he is very bad at math.

When Danny learns that the man at the public library who has been recommending books for him to read for the last two months is Mr. Malter, he is just as surprised as Reuven is. Here, then, is proof that Mr. Malter *does* know more about Danny than he let on to his son. We understand better Mr. Malter's previous insistence that Reuven make Danny a friend. Reuven can help Danny become more comfortable living in a secular, less strictly religious world; Danny can help Reuven broaden his own world view by introducing him to Hasidism. Their friendship symbolizes the hope that the two religious positions that they represent can be reconciled. Likewise, Mr. Malter's position as the person who has been recommending books to Danny also suggests that the two religious schools of thought can be reconciled.

- **clop**   a colloquialism for a physical blow.
- **hit the canvas**   to be knocked down in a boxing ring.
- **kosher**   an adjective describing Kashrut, the Jewish dietary laws. These laws require that animals intended for food be killed by specially trained men in such a manner that the animal feels little pain, that dairy and meat dishes not be prepared or eaten at the same time, and that certain animals not be eaten. Following these dietary laws, which come from the Torah, is one of the ways in which Jewish people retain their identity.
- **prelim man**   a less skilled fighter who boxes in matches staged before the main fight.
- **abba**   (ah bah) Hebrew word for father; a term of endearment.
- **tefillin**   (tuh fill in) A religious accessory used by Jewish men in morning prayer service, it consists of small boxes, containing Biblical quotations, attached to each other with strips of leather that the person praying winds around his hand and places upon his head as a symbolic binding of himself to God.
- **Caen and Carentan**   cities in northwestern France.
- **Isle of Wight**   a British island in the English Channel.
- **Normandy**   a region in northwestern France where Allied troops landed on D-Day (June 6, 1944) during World War II.
- **Royal Air Force bombers**   British planes or pilots who drop bombs.
- **cockeyed**   askew; slightly crazy.
- **phylacteries**   (fill lack tuh rees) like tefillin (listed previously), objects used during Jewish prayer.
- **blatt**   a page of Talmud.

- **Kiddushin** (Key do sheen) a book of the Talmud.

- **Maimonidean** (My mon uh day on) a reference to the great Jewish medieval scholar Maimonides.

- *Ivanhoe* a novel set in the Middle Ages, by English author Sir Walter Scott (1771-1832).

- **Darwin** Charles Darwin (1809-82), an English naturalist who theorized that humankind evolved from "lower" species.

- **Huxley** Thomas Henry Huxley (1825-95), an English educator and biologist who championed Darwinism and agnosticism.

- **dynasty** a succession of powerful rulers, often from the same family.

- **Russell and Whitehead** Bertrand Russell (1872-1970) and Alfred Whitehead (1861-1947), authors of the three-volume book *Principia Mathematica*, considered a landmark in the study of logic.

- **agitated** emotionally and physically disturbed.

BOOK TWO

CHAPTERS 5-7

Summary

Reuven is happy to be home from the hospital and looks forward to resuming the observance of the Sabbath. He asks his father to explain Danny's particular sect of Judaism, Hasidism. To do that, Mr. Malter relates the history of the founding of Hasidism.

Finishing the story, Mr. Malter informs Reuven that Reb Saunders is a tzaddik with a reputation for brilliance and compassion. And just as Reb Saunders inherited the position from his father, so will the position go to Danny.

Mr. Malter tells Reuven that he has a brilliant mind but that Danny is a "phenomenon." He says that he is happy that Reuven and Danny have become friends. Because of his great intelligence, Danny is terribly torn and lonely. Their friendship cannot but help both of them.

Waking up from a nap one Saturday afternoon after Sabbath services, Reuven sees Danny standing before him. Danny says that his father, Reb Saunders, wants to meet Reuven, so they set off for Danny's synagogue, which is on the first floor of the Saunders family home. The boys exchange information about their families. Reuven tells Danny that his mother died soon after he was born. Danny has a younger brother and sister. He says that his family came from Russia and that the family name, *Senders*, was Americanized by immigration officials to *Saunders*.

At the synagogue, Danny introduces Reuven to his father, who asks how Reuven's eye is healing.

Reb Saunders leads the Sabbath service; then, after he and the male members of the congregation eat, he gives a sort of sermon, incorporating passages and commentary on the Talmud. Then, as in some Jewish households where the son is at a yeshiva and the father is a learned man, Reb Saunders quizzes his son on his knowledge of Jewish history and teachings, in what seems to Reuven to be a sort of contest. Reuven is drawn into the contest when Reb Saunders asks him to find the error in a mathematical aspect of his sermon.

Speaking to Reuven after the service, Reb Saunders compliments Mr. Malter as a great scholar, whose work, however, he does not agree with. He expresses pleasure that Danny and Reuven are friends.

Commentary

In Chapter 5, Reuven seems to be reborn metaphorically when he returns home with his father from the hospital. He notices details that he never before took the time to recognize, including the hydrangea bush, which he calls a "snowball bush," in his front yard. He comments, "I had never really paid any attention to it before. Now it seemed suddenly luminous and alive." Walking through the apartment, he thinks to himself, "I had lived in it all my life, but I never really saw it until I went through it that Friday afternoon." Reuven's rediscovery of the objects and setting that, together, constitute his everyday life recalls his father's wise words while Reuven was still in the hospital: Fortune is best when we have experienced misfortune. This sudden clarity of vision also demonstrates that Reuven is beginning to open his eyes and become aware of the world outside of his own existence.

Potok devotes Chapter 6 to explaining the historical background of Hasidism, of which Danny and his father are members.

Notable in Mr. Malter's discussion of Jewish history is his explanation of pilpul—in his words, "empty, nonsensical arguments over minute points of the Talmud that have no relationship at all to the world." Because Mr. Malter is concerned with world events, we expect him to have an unfavorable opinion of pilpul. Likewise, because Reb Saunders is concerned not with secular ideas but only with Judaism, we expect him to be very familiar with and practice pilpul. (This expectation is confirmed in Chapter 7.)

Mr. Malter's history lesson in Chapter 6 also concerns Danny, whom Mr. Malter likens to a historical figure name Maimon. Maimon, eager for knowledge in addition to that contained in the Talmud, studied many world-famous philosophers. Mr. Malter says of him, "He wanted to know what was happening in the outside world." Comparing Danny to Maimon, Mr. Malter notes of Reuven's friend, "But he is a phenomenon. Once in a generation is a mind like that born." However, given his intellectual prowess, Danny is lonely, torn between what is expected of him and what he himself wants to do. Knowing that this conflict exists in Danny, Mr. Malter again commends Reuven for befriending Danny. Concluding his discussion with Reuven, Mr. Malter reaffirms his philosophical belief, "That is the way the world is."

Chapter 7 continues the history lesson from the preceding chapter. This time, however, Danny, not Mr. Malter, is Reuven's history teacher. Danny's father led his followers from Russia to the United States in 1918, following persecution by Russian Cossacks. Reb Saunders and his followers eventually settled in the Williamsburg section of Brooklyn, where, in 1929, Danny and Reuven were born, two days apart, in the same hospital. Incredibly, Danny and Reuven live only five blocks from each other, yet they meet for the first time at the ballgame that begins the novel.

Accompanying Danny to his father's shul for religious service allows Reuven to experience a new world: Hasidism. Potok details the setting within Reb Saunders' home, and especially the first floor, which serves as the meeting place for the Reb and his followers. This room seems starkly bare. The walls and ceiling are painted white, the floor is bare wood, and light bulbs hanging from the ceiling are exposed, producing a "harsh light." We see the Hasidim celebrating the Sabbath and get an idea of Danny

Saunders' world, a world devoted to God and the Torah. Danny is completely at home in this environment, even if he wants to extend his world to include studying the secular area of psychology. Understandably, Reuven is not comfortable in Danny's world. As Reuven says, "I just couldn't get it through my head that Danny had to go through something like that every week."

When Reb Saunders briefly meets Reuven in the hall for the first time, his concern about Reuven centers more on Reuven's father than on Reuven, as he asks, "You are the son of David Malter?" The more usual question would be, "*Are you* the son of David Malter?" Instead, Reb Saunders changes the order of the first two words, emphasizing his commanding presence and power and implying that he knows the answer already. Later in this brief encounter, Reb Saunders says, "A son of David Malter surely knows Hebrew." He knows of Reuven through Reuven's father, just like Mr. Malter knows of Danny through Danny's father.

Reb Saunders' speech following the meal after the religious service includes much history. His narration completes that started by Mr. Malter in Chapter 6 and continued by Danny toward the beginning of Chapter 7. In his speech, Reb Saunders includes teachings based on gematriya, in which each letter of the Hebrew alphabet designates a number, so that every Hebrew word has a numerical value. Reb Saunders also practices a form of pilpul with Danny, although Reuven realizes that "it wasn't really pilpul, they weren't twisting the texts out of shape, they seemed more interested in . . . straightforward knowledge and simple explanations." Then Reb Saunders asks Reuven his opinion of the gematriya, knowing that one example that he discussed was added incorrectly and trusting Reuven's mathematical abilities to decipher the correct numerical value. Here, Reb Saunders tests Reuven's intellectual abilities to reassure himself that Reuven will be a good, competent friend for Danny.

Reuven and his father's conversation about Reuven's visit to Danny's emphasizes once again Mr. Malter's philosophy of life, which is so different from Reb Saunders'. Speaking of Reb Saunders, Mr. Malter says, "It is a pity he occupies his mind only with Talmud. . . . But he lives only in his own world," cut off from the larger society that surrounds him. Mr. Malter expects that Danny, once he assumes his father's religious position, will behave as Danny's father does, shutting off his mind from the secular world. Danny and Reuven have become good friends, but they still live in different worlds. Ironically, Mr. Malter's expectations of Danny foreshadow the end of the novel, but in the opposite way. That is, Danny will *not* shut off his mind from the outside world.

- **row houses** houses having common walls with the houses on either side; this type of housing is often found in older urban areas in the United States.

- **Herzl** (**Her** tsul) Theodor Herzl (1860-1904), Austrian founder of a modern movement known as Zionism, whose goal was to create a Jewish state.

- **Bialik** (Bee **al** lick) Hayyim Nahman Bialik (1873-1934), a Jewish poet who had a decisive influence on the renaissance of the Hebrew language in the late nineteenth and twentieth centuries.

- **Chaim Weizmann** (1874-1952) a Zionist leader and first president of the state of Israel.

- **ailanthus tree** a tree with bitter-scented flowers, usually found in the tropics.

- **pilpul** (**pill** pull) the dry, stale manner of Jewish study in seventeenth- and eighteenth-century Europe that inspired the rise of Hasidism.

- **tallit** (**tal** leet) a shawl used by Jews in prayer.

- **shofar** (**show** far) an ancient ritual horn of Israel, used to announce important public events.

- **beadle** a minor church official in charge of ushering and keeping order during religious services.

- **amulets** objects or charms superstitiously worn to ward off evil.

- **Kaddish** (**Cad** ish) the Jewish prayer for the departed.

- **Benedict de Spinoza** (1632-77) Dutch Jewish philosopher.

- **Liebniz** Gottfried Wilhelm Liebniz (1646-1716), German mathematician.

- **Hume** David Hume (1711-76), Scottish philosopher.

- **Immanual Kant** (1724-1804) German philosopher.

- **caftan** (**calf** tan) a long coat worn by the Hasidim.

- **scythe**   an instrument with a long blade and long handle used for cutting grass.

- **Eternal Light**   a symbol in the synagogue that symbolizes the permanence of the Torah and the radiance of the Jewish faith.

- **gefilte fish**   (guh fill tuh) cakes or balls of seasoned fish.

- **catechism**   a written record of religious beliefs, usually in a question-and-answer format.

- **din**   overwhelming noise.

- **ascribe**   credit with.

- **vestibule**   entryway.

- **nu**   a Jewish colloquial expression meaning "so" or "so then" or "and then what?"

- **gematriya**   (gem ot ree ya) a sort of arithmetical amusement to disclose the hidden meaning of biblical or other text by determining the numerical equivalents of the Hebrew letters in a Hebrew word.

- **Mitnagdim**   (Meet **nog** dim) critics or opponents of the Hasidic way of life.

- **secular**   not specifically religious.

CHAPTERS 8-10

Summary

Danny meets Reuven at the library and reads from Heinrich Graetz's *History of the Jews*, a history book that is uncomplimentary (and not totally accurate, Mr. Malter later tells Reuven) about Hasidic Judaism. Danny tells Reuven that the picture of Hasidim in Graetz's account is totally alien to what he knows but is distressing nonetheless. Danny then launches into a discussion of psychology, talking about the unconscious, about dreams, and about Sigmund Freud, a pioneer in the field of psychology, known as the father of psychoanalysis.

Later in the evening, Reuven mentions to his father that Danny reads a lot of Freud. Impressed, Mr. Malter says that he feels a little guilty about giving Danny books behind his father's back but does so because Danny would have sought these books eventually anyway.

At the Saunders' house, Reb Saunders, Danny, and Reuven study *Pirkei Avot (Ethics of the Fathers)* on Shabbat. While Danny is downstairs getting some tea for them, the Reb talks to Reuven about Danny.

Reb Saunders says that he knows that Danny has been going to the library and wants Reuven to tell him what Danny has been reading. In a very moving speech about Danny, Reb Saunders says that his son is his most precious possession.

Reuven realizes that he has to tell Reb Saunders how Danny met his father and what books Mr. Malter has suggested that Danny read, and he does so. (However, he does not tell the Reb that Danny is teaching himself German, that he plans to read Freud, and that he has read some books on Hasidism.) Reb Saunders is shocked and bewildered at these revelations. He laments to God that he has a brilliant son, but does he have to be *so* brilliant?

After the meeting with Reb Saunders, Reuven tells Danny that he told his father everything, and Danny replies that his father would have found out about it all anyway. He says that Reb Saunders and he do not talk—except during study time, his father is mostly silent toward him.

Back home, Reuven tells his father about Danny being raised in silence. Neither Reuven nor his father can understand why Reb and Danny cannot communicate with each other.

Commentary

When Reuven returns to school for the first time after the ballgame accident, his classmates treat him as a hero. Potok again emphasizes Reuven's new outlook on life and his newfound awareness of the world around him. Reuven comments, "So many things had happened, and everything looked so different." Later, when he visits Danny in the public library, Reuven sees things he's never before taken the time to notice, including the murals on the library's interior walls. What catches his attention the most is a mural depicting Homer, whose eyes seem "glazed, almost without pupils, as if the artist had been trying to show that he had been blind." Reuven's comments about Homer's blind-looking eyes recall the time Reuven spent in the hospital and the concern he has for Billy, the young blind boy with whom he shared a room. Reuven no longer takes his eyesight—and, by extension, his life and the people in it—for granted, as he did before the ballgame.

Reuven and Danny's conversation in the public library centers around Danny's reading Hasidic history and learning German so that he can study Freud's original writings on psychology. After reading Graetz's *History of the Jews*, Danny is horrified that Graetz contends that Hasidic Jews are drunkards. Although he knows that Graetz is wrong about this contention, he internalizes the negative picture of Hasidism that Graetz paints in the book. When Reuven counters that Graetz's writing is only one version and therefore not to be trusted completely, Danny ignores Reuven's comment. Reuven narrates about Danny, "I had the feeling he was talking more to himself than to me." Later, when Reuven summarizes his conversation with Danny for his father, Mr. Malter is especially saddened by Danny's choice of subject. "The unconscious and dreams," Mr. Malter contemplates. "And Freud. At the age of fifteen." Here, Mr. Malter is concerned that, although Danny has the intellect to study Freud's theories of psychology, Danny does not have the emotional maturity necessary to accept or reject valid arguments concerning both Hasidism and Freudian psychology. As Mr. Malter says after Reuven and Danny meet again at the library, "Freud is not God in psychology."

Reuven's second visit to Danny's house to study with Danny and Reb Saunders allows Reuven to describe the living quarters on the brownstone's second and third floors. The family, except for Danny, live on the second floor; Danny's bedroom is on the third floor, along with his father's study. Reuven notes that the walls and ceilings of the brownstone's second and third floors are white, without any pictures hanging on them. The stark setting's lack of personal touches such as family photographs parallels Danny's growing up in silence—the lack of a shared, personal language with his father.

The Talmudic discussion between Danny and his father is heated and confrontational, to the point that Reuven thinks that they might physically hit each other. However, their arguing is also ritualistic in that each knows the strategies of the other in discussing the Talmud; these sessions occur regularly. Reuven, finally understanding that the contest between father and son is friendly yet competitive, notes "an ease about them, an intimacy." He also realizes that Reb Saunders is most proud of and happy with Danny when Danny bests his father concerning Talmudic interpretation. Ironically, then, Reb Saunders demonstrates the love he feels for his son by challenging him about Talmudic meaning rather than affectionately showing his love in a more traditional fashion, as Mr. Malter does with Reuven.

Reb Saunders reveals even more about himself when he discusses with Reuven the affection that he has for his son while Danny is downstairs getting tea. Because Reb Saunders believes that his son should be raised in silence except when discussing the Talmud or religious topics, he has never told Danny that he loves him. Acknowledging that he is well aware that Danny is reading secular material but that he will not—cannot—talk to Danny about it, he says to Reuven, "My son is my most precious possession. I have nothing in the world compared to my son." What is most baffling at this point in the novel is why Reb Saunders will not tell his son that he loves him, why he will not even *talk* to his son except about religion.

Walking back home with Danny following his visit with Reb Saunders, Reuven asks Danny why his father does not speak to him. Danny is as perplexed about his father's refusal as is Reuven: "My father believes in silence. . . . He told me to stop running to him every time I had a problem."

Once Reuven returns home and speaks to his father about Danny's father's silence, Reuven gains a better understanding of why Reb Saunders wanted to speak to him alone, without Danny in the room. Mr. Malter explains to Reuven that Reb Saunders spoke to Reuven *knowing* that Reuven would then speak to Danny. In this way, Reb Saunders has spoken to his son. However, Potok leaves unanswered as yet *why* Reb Saunders deals with his son in silence. Reb Saunders cannot talk openly with Danny, but Mr. Malter has open, warm communication with Reuven. Potok again shows us the different worlds in which Reuven and Danny live. Yet they are capable of a nurturing friendship.

The brief Chapter 9 centers on Reuven's calling Billy Merrit, the boy with whom he shared a hospital room, and learning from Billy's father that the surgery performed on Billy's eyes was unsuccessful. Billy probably will be blind for the rest of his life.

Despondent over the news about Billy, Reuven wanders aimlessly about the apartment. Note the many references to Reuven's heightened senses. For example, his hands *feel* very cold, he *sees* sunlight hitting the leaves of an ailanthus tree—nicknamed the tree of heaven—outside a window and *smells* its "musty odor," and he *hears* a fly buzzing. The incident in which he frees the fly from the spider web perhaps suggests Reuven's emotional reaction upon learning Billy's fate. Billy cannot do anything to change his sightless condition. Reuven, emotionally upset about the lack of control that Billy has over his future, assures that the tiniest of creatures *does* have a future, at least a temporary one. Freeing the fly from the spider web is Reuven's metaphorical attempt to free Billy of his blindness, which, of course, he knows he cannot.

The war news that opens Chapter 10 reminds us of the historical situation that serves as a background to the novel. Reuven and his father diligently follow the news; Danny is too caught up in studying the Talmud to pay attention to world events.

Danny has difficulty learning German in order to read Freud in the original because of the various meanings that German words can have. He frets over one text's translation of a German word compared to another text's translation of the same word. What Danny wants most is for a word to have only one meaning. His outlook on life is based solely on everything being either right or wrong, with no middle ground for compromise. This world view contrasts with Mr. Malter's view, "That is the way the world is." Mr. Malter accepts that things in the world are not usually completely right or completely wrong; Danny does not.

Danny's breakthrough in reading Freud occurs when he realizes that Freud has to be *studied*, not simply read. He applies the methods he uses to study the Talmud to learning Freud. Although this breakthrough may seem insignificant, it demonstrates that Danny is maturing beyond a wholly religious outlook on life. He is now able to use the knowledge he gains through studying religious topics and apply it to more secular areas of study.

Chapter 10 ends on a somber tone. The summer is over, and Reuven and his father return to the city from their summer vacation; Danny has spent the entire summer studying the Talmud and Freud. Although Reuven and Danny promise each other that they will get together to discuss their summer activities, school begins, and neither one has free time. To a great extent, the end of the chapter foreshadows the boys' separation at the end of the novel.

- **Ionic columns** A feature of Greek architecture, an Ionic column is grooved and set on a base.

- **conjunction** in logic, a statement that is true if and only if each of its parts is true.

- **disjunction** in logic, two statements joined with the word *or*.

- **equivalence** in logic, a relationship between two statements such that either both are true or neither is.

- **deductive** a system of reasoning that works on the premise of "if A, then B" to find the relationships between premises.

- **draw nigh** approach; come near.

- **pilgrimage** a journey to a sacred place.

- **incumbent** obligatory.

- **perversities** corruptions.

- **allusions** indirect references.

- **gall** insulting boldness.

- **goy** a Jewish colloquial term for a non-Jew.

- **Sanhedrin** (San **head** rin) a book in the Talmud.

- **Avodah Zarah** a book in the Talmud dealing with idolatry and superstitions.

- **Baba Bathra** a book in the Talmud.

- **Rashi** a medieval commentator on the Torah and the Talmud.

- **Cassell's** a brand of comprehensive language dictionaries, available in French, Spanish, German, and other languages. Danny uses the German one to assist him in reading Freud.

- **La-Haye-du-Prits** a city in France.

- **panzer**   a World War II German tank.
- **Vire**   a river in northwestern France.
- **St.-Lô**   a community in northwestern France.
- **lodgment area**   the place where soldiers spend the night.
- **Theodore Dreiser**   (1871-1945) American novelist.

CHAPTERS 11 & 12

Summary

Reb Saunders, Danny, and Reuven learn that a major German offensive has been repelled in the Battle of the Bulge and that the Allies apparently will win the war. Americans, along with the rest of the world, mourn the murder of millions of Jews slaughtered by Hitler. Reb Saunders speaks of the European Jews he had known who are probably dead, of the brutality of the world, of his years in Russia with Cossack bands looting and plundering, and now, of the monstrosity of Hitler and the Nazis.

Reuven and his father discuss Reb Saunders' opinion that the Holocaust must be the result of divine will. Mr. Malter disagrees and says that because millions of Jews were murdered needlessly, they cannot wait for the Messiah to come or for other help in creating a Jewish state. Jews must do the work themselves.

Mr. Malter suffers a heart attack. During his convalescence at the hospital, Danny and his family invite Reuven to stay at their house, and he accepts. Danny and Reuven spend much time at the library, especially discussing the ideas of Freud. Reuven thinks that Freud's theories are hardly complimentary to a religious person, so he finds it odd that Danny seems to have accepted Freud's ideas. To Reuven, Talmudic ideals and Freudian ideas cannot coexist. However, when he tells this to Danny, Danny says nothing and goes back to his reading.

One morning during breakfast in the Saunders' house, Reuven says that a lot of people are saying that it is time for Palestine (the current state of Israel) to become a Jewish homeland and not only a place where pious Jews go do die. Reb Saunders becomes enraged at Reuven and leaves the table, visibly upset. Later, Danny tells Reuven not to talk about a Jewish state in front of his father, who takes God and Torah very seriously. A secular Jewish state to the Reb is a sacrilege, a violation of the Torah.

Commentary

The beginning of Chapter 11 continues the somber tone of Chapter 10. School begins for Reuven and Danny, and they are too busy with schoolwork to talk in person, although they talk often on the telephone. Reuven says that he and Danny never get to discuss Danny's reading Freud, a comment he also made in Chapter 10. All Reuven knows is that Danny's reading has upset Danny. Without someone with whom to discuss what he's studying, Danny apparently is becoming depressed and retreating even further from the secular world than before he and Reuven became friends. For example, when Reuven calls Danny following the end of the Battle of the Bulge, in January 1945, and asks him what he thinks about the battle, Danny answers "vaguely" and immediately wants to know when he and Reuven can get together.

President Roosevelt's death on April 12, 1945, has a deep emotional effect on Reuven, as it does on everyone in his community. Ironically, Roosevelt's death, sad though it is, also has a positive effect on Reuven, although whether or not he is aware of this positive effect is questionable: He matures as a character because he is forced to deal with grief. By equating Roosevelt's death with Billy's blindness, he finally is able to give a name to his feeling concerning Billy's blindness, a feeling that he has struggled to name since learning that Billy will be blind forever: senselessness. Reuven muses about the president's death, "It was senseless, as—I held my breath, feeling myself shiver with fear—as Billy's blindness was senseless. That was it. It was as senseless, as empty of meaning, as Billy's blindness." The sentence "That was it" in this quoted passage signifies Reuven's growth as a character. He now understands something about himself that he did not recognize before.

One of the greatest contrasts between Reb Saunders and David Malter in the novel is their individual reactions on learning of the inconceivable number of Jews killed in the German concentration camps during World War II. "How the world makes us suffer," Reb Saunders says to Reuven and Danny. "It is the will of God. We must accept the will of God." Because the horror of the deaths is incomprehensible to Reb Saunders, he concludes that the killings are God's will; if God had not let the Holocaust happen, it wouldn't have. He can do nothing but accept that this is God's will. David Malter's reaction is as emotionally strong as Reb Saunders', but he assumes an active role in defining what should now happen following the mass killings. When Reuven tells his father about Reb Saunders' comments concerning God's will, Mr. Malter responds, "We cannot wait for God. If there is an answer, we must make it ourselves. . . . It will have meaning only if we give it meaning." Because Mr. Malter believes that Jews should interact with the secular world, we expect him to take an active role in Jewish world affairs. Likewise, because Reb Saunders' philosophy of life is completely grounded in Hasidism, we expect him to insulate himself within his religion and leave world affairs to the will of God.

Chapter 11 ends in a somber tone, as did Chapter 10. David Malter suffers a heart attack, and Reuven temporarily moves in with Danny's family while his father recuperates.

Reuven's stay with Danny's family allows us to gain a better insight into the Saunders family. Reb Saunders is both physically and emotionally devastated by the slaughter of millions of Jews during World War II. Dark circles form around his eyes, and he walks perpetually bent over. Reuven notes that Reb Saunders is "forever silent, withdrawn, his eyes turned inward, brooding, as if witnessing a sea of suffering he alone could see." Danny's father appears to be internalizing the suffering of his people. Reuven also is concerned that Danny and his father never communicate with each other, as if they are "physically incapable" of speaking warm words of affection.

Danny continues to struggle intellectually and emotionally with much of what he reads concerning Freud. He acknowledges Freud's knowledge of human nature, but he cannot reconcile within himself the less-than-flattering opinion Freud has of humanity, especially given the Holocaust. Reuven says of Freud's theory of human nature and Danny's attempts to understand it, "It tore man from God, as Danny put it, and married him off to Satan." Even Reuven is troubled by the relationship between Freud and religion. However, when he wants to discuss the subject,

Danny refuses to do so, as if he alone carries the burden of reconciling Freud and God. Danny's internalizing this burden reminds us of Reb Saunders' carrying all the suffering of his people.

The issue of establishing a Jewish homeland in Palestine is as contentious a matter between David Malter and Reb Saunders as the Holocaust is. In his hospital bed, recuperating from his heart attack, Mr. Malter tells his son and Danny that Jews cannot wait for God to send a messiah to solve the world's—specifically the Jews'—problems. Jews must act now and establish a Jewish homeland. The only hope that Jews have rests on American Jewry. Reb Saunders, speaking to his family and Reuven one night at supper, emphatically disagrees with Mr. Malter's opinion, although he does not know that Mr. Malter has spoken to Reuven and Danny. Reb Saunders' position is that God—not Jews or any people, all of whom are sinful—is responsible for establishing a Jewish homeland. When God deems that the right time has come for such a homeland, a messiah will come and establish it.

Danny and Reuven's conversation in Chapter 12 concerning first Danny's brother, then Danny's sister, then Danny's father, and finally Danny himself foreshadows Danny's decision to reject the inherited position of leader of his Hasidic community at the end of the novel. Danny reveals very personal information that he has never revealed before to Reuven. For example, he says that he pities his younger brother. However, he is also dependent on his brother in that his future decision not to accept his inherited religious position will be easier to make knowing that his brother can assume the position. His comment that his sister is already promised in marriage stops any intention Reuven might have about dating her. Danny's trusting that his father's motives for demanding silence between them is ironic: Although Danny says that his father is a great man and therefore must have valid reasons not to speak to him, he also comments that his father is intellectually "trapped," which Danny refuses to become. He admires his father but does not want to live his life like him.

• **Battle of the Bulge** a month-long battle (December 1944 to January 1945) in the Ardennes region of northeast France during which the Allies succeeded in holding off German troops and hastened the end of the war in Europe.

46

- **Kôënigsberg**   the easternmost city of the German empire; after World War II, it became part of the Soviet Union and was renamed Kalingrad.

- **Breslau**   a city in Germany.

- **Rhine**   a river that runs through west-central Germany.

- **Remagen**   the German city where Allied troops crossed the Rhine River to capture Cologne near the end of World War II.

- **sulfa**   a bacteria-inhibiting drug.

- **cerebral hemorrhage**   severe bleeding of the brain.

- **House of Commons**   one of two legislative bodies of the British government (the other is the House of Lords).

- **R. Anthony Eden**   (1897-1977) British statesman and prime minister (1955-57).

- **Wailing Wall**   the holiest place in the world for a religious Jew. The Wailing Wall is the last remnant of the Jewish temple that was destroyed by the Romans in the year 70 A.D. Jews hold many types of religious services there.

- **Eretz Yisroel**   (Eh retz Yees rah ale) Hebrew for the land of Israel.

- **goyishkeit**   (goy ish kite) a Jewish colloquial word referring to the culture of a non-Jew.

BOOK THREE

CHAPTERS 13-15

Summary

Danny and Reuven enter Hirsch College. To his dismay, Danny soon learns that the college psychology department is oriented toward experimental psychology to the exclusion of the psychoanalytic work of Freud. The school is, in Jewish practice, Orthodox.

Mr. Malter is busy giving talks on the importance of the Zionist movement (the movement to create a Jewish state). He speaks at a rally at Madison Square Garden for the Zionist cause. The rally is a great success, and the response to the idea of an end to British control of Palestine and the establishment of a Jewish state there is overwhelming.

The rally, including Mr. Malter's participation in it, is reported in the press. Angered by the rally and Mr. Malter's call for a Jewish state, Reb Saunders cannot sanction his son associating with Reuven, the son of a Zionist leader. Accordingly, he forbids Danny to see or speak to Reuven.

In November 1947, the United Nations votes to partition Palestine into a Jewish state and an Arab state.

Commentary

The confrontation between David Malter and Reb Saunders about religious ideology spills over into Reuven and Danny's college life. Reuven is friendly with the non-Hasidic students, many of whom he went to high school with, but he doesn't "mix much" with the Hasidic students. Likewise, Danny befriends the Hasidic students but not the non-Hasidic ones. Each group of students confronts the other concerning the question of a Jewish homeland in Palestine. Their conflict parallels that between David Malter and Reb Saunders.

Reuven and Danny's heated discussion about the value of experimental psychology and Freud reveals their respective world views. Reuven argues that Freudians aren't willing to test their theories in the real world; therefore, their theories are merely assumptions. Later in Chapter 13, Professor Appleman, Danny's psychology professor, emphasizes to Danny that Freud might have been a genius, but he based his theories only on *abnormal* human behavior. Danny is unable to accept Reuven's and Appleman's arguments: Human behavior does not concern him; psychological behavior does. Here, Danny's opinion is ironic given the recent information about the great number of Jews killed in the German concentration camps. Finally, however, after speaking to Appleman about his concerns, Danny begins to accept the validity of experimental psychology. This acceptance furthers his development, or maturity, as a character.

We learn much about David Malter in Chapter 13, especially his motivation for driving himself so hard to make a difference in the world. Speaking to Reuven, who has matured greatly in a short period, Mr. Malter says, "A man must fill his life with meaning, meaning not automatically given in life." Using a metaphor of an eye that blinks, he explains that the blink is nothing; it is only a physical function. However, the eye itself *is* important, for the eye symbolizes humanity in that it has a deeper meaning than simply something that blinks. Furthering this analogy, Mr. Malter contends that a human life in and of itself is inconsequential; however, what a human being *does* can be very important if that human being makes a difference in the world. Note that Mr. Malter relies on eyesight in his metaphor of an eye being like a human being. We are reminded of his fear for Reuven's eyesight after Reuven gets hit by a ball earlier in the novel, and also of his extreme sadness when he first sees Billy, Reuven's roommate in the hospital, and realizes that Billy cannot see.

Danny broods more and more, as if he were contemplating a weighty issue in his life (which we know is the question of whether to renounce his inherited religious position). He refrains from joining the pro-Jewish homeland students, but he also removes himself from any discussion among the Hasidic students, who are against a Jewish homeland. Reuven relates Danny's position: "He was trapped by his beard and earlocks, he said, and there was nothing he could do. But one day . . ." Here, the phrase "But one day," followed as it is by an ellipsis, foreshadows Danny's momentous decision at the end of the novel to decline the inherited rabbinical leadership.

Worse, Reb Saunders forbids Danny to have any contact with Reuven because of Reuven's father's public statements concerning the Palestinian Jewish homeland. In effect, then, Reb Saunders silences Danny completely. Danny cannot speak to his father, and now he cannot speak to his friend.

At the end of Chapter 13, Mr. Malter responds to Reuven's outcry about Reb Saunders—"He's such a—a fanatic!"—by pointing out that were there not such men as Reb Saunders, Jews would no longer exist, for they would have been erased as a people. Here, Mr. Malter exhibits such an even-tempered and understanding philosophy of life that we marvel at him as a character.

Chapter 14 is noteworthy for Reuven's extended explanation of a Talmudic passage in class. His four-day answer comes on the heels of silence, both between him and Danny and in class. One of his strongest statements concerning silence occurs early in the chapter: "Silence was ugly, it was black, it leered, it was cancerous, it was death." Responding to this characterization of silence and the enforced silence between him and his best friend, Reuven launches into his one-sided discussion about the Talmudic passage. However, when Rav Gershenson, the teacher, asks Reuven what *he*, and not the historical commentators, thinks is the meaning of the passage, Reuven is speechless, for he cannot explain its meaning. Not even Rav Gershenson can explain. Here, then, Reuven is faced with something that cannot be given meaning, which reminds us of his father's previous comment that a person gains fulfillment by creating meaning out of life experiences. Reuven learns that some questions have no answers. No doubt Danny, too, who is in Reuven's Talmudic class, learns the same lesson.

At the end of Chapter 15, Reuven and Danny reconcile. Because of the political and military turmoil in Israel, Reb Saunders must have rescinded his order that Danny not interact with Reuven, or perhaps Danny personally decided to disobey his father's decree of silence concerning Reuven. Whichever the reason, the two boys—men now—again speak to one another. Their silence and then reunion demonstrate that world events *do* make a difference in Reb Saunders' life, although perhaps Reb Saunders would not admit that the secular world impacts his life as much as it does.

- **induction** in logic, arriving at a general conclusion by looking at particular instances.

- **refutation** proving that something is wrong through argument and evidence.

- **intersubjective testing** testing to get the same results from two or more subjects.

- **emendation** a change (usually of text) to correct or improve.

- **empiricist** a person who believes that knowledge is gained only through experience.

- **Neturei Karta** (Net u rye Car tuh) an ultra-Orthodox Jewish group in Jerusalem.

- **British Foreign Minister Bevin** Ernest Bevin (1881-1951), who served as England's foreign secretary from 1945 to 1951.

- **rostrum** a podium used by speakers or lecturers.

- **shiur** (shee **ur**) a Jewish classroom lesson.
- **Haganah** (Hah gah **nah**) a military organization of Israel.

CHAPTERS 16-18

Summary

Danny resumes talking to Reuven, and the boys apologize to one another. Danny has resigned himself to experimental psychology and wants to study for a Ph.D. He dreads telling his father about this plan, but is intent on going through with it.

Reuven tells his father of Danny's plans to study psychology in graduate school and thus give up the position of tzaddik that he was to inherit from his father. Mr. Malter says that this decision is going to cause Reb Saunders a lot of pain.

Reuven asks Danny if he will still practice Orthodox Judaism when he goes to graduate school, and Danny replies that nothing will prevent him from keeping the tradition. Danny is accepted into Columbia University and is apprehensive about telling his father but knows that he has to. He procrastinates.

Reuven visits the Saunders home for the first day of Passover. Reb Saunders, Danny, and Reuven talk. Reb Saunders speaks to Danny through Reuven. The Reb discusses how he himself was raised in silence and the reasons for his continuing this practice with Danny. In addition, he knows all about Danny's academic intentions and discharges him from his responsibilities as a tzaddik, acknowledging that Danny will be a "tzaddik for the world."

Danny and Reuven graduate from Hirsch College, and Danny leaves to go to Columbia University. He and Reuven vow to continue their friendship.

Commentary

At the start of Chapter 16, Reuven and Danny discuss their period of forced silence. Reuven's statement "Welcome back to the land of the living" suggests that silence equals death, a theme further emphasized when we recall Mr. Malter's comments concerning the world's refusal to do anything that might have prevented the Holocaust. Although the silence between Reuven and Danny was not as drastic as Danny and his father's extended silence, Reuven learns from the experience that he hates not being able to communicate with his friend. When he asks Danny how Danny copes with his father's lack of communication, Danny can only respond, "You learn to live with it." Danny has no choice but to accept his father's decision not to talk to him except when studying the Talmud.

We now know that Reb Saunders and not Danny himself decided that Danny could once again talk to Reuven, for Danny says, "The ban has been lifted." What we do not yet know is *why* Reb Saunders demands silence from his son. Mr. Malter comments to Reuven, "What a price to pay for a soul," but he does not clarify this statement.

Danny's decision to enter the field of clinical psychology demonstrates his continuing maturity. He no longer accepts the blanket statement that Freud is God, nor does he embrace experimental psychology. Instead, he finds a middle ground between Freud and experimentation in clinical psychology. He determines to study humans, not rats.

The climax of the novel—Danny's telling his father that he does not want to become the rabbinic leader of his community—is foreshadowed when Reuven asks Danny if Reb Saunders knows of his future plans. Reb Saunders learns about his son's decision *after* Danny receives his rabbinic ordination.

The first scene in Chapter 17 emphasizes Potok's theme of silence once again. However, silence now becomes more than an absence of language or, as Reuven stressed in the preceding chapter, an equivalent of death, for Danny says that "you can listen to silence and learn from it." Ironically, silence "talks." Here, Danny suggests that silence enables a person to more deeply ponder the suffering of people in the world. By remaining silent, a person can hear other people's cries for help and understanding. A person who *talks* about problems hears only his or her own words, but a person who is *quiet* hears the pleadings of others because that person ponders the "pain of the world."

Much of Chapter 17 prepares the reader—and Danny—for the climactic confrontation between Danny and his father over Danny's plans to reject his inherited rabbinic position and study to become a clinical psychologist. Mr. Malter is most concerned that

Danny plan out exactly what he will tell his father. Reuven's father again refuses to tell Reuven the reasons for Reb Saunders' silence toward Danny, although he obviously has some understanding of Reb Saunders' motivations. He rhetorically questions Reuven concerning Hasids, "Why must they feel the burden of the world is only on their shoulders?" and later in the chapter directly asks Danny if Danny can *hear* the silence, which Danny said earlier that he can.

Reb Saunders' repeatedly asking Danny to invite Reuven over to the Saunders home suggests that Danny's father has something to discuss with Reuven: Danny. We expect Reb Saunders to speak to his son about his son's behavior and future plans *through* Reuven, as he did in Chapter 8 when he wanted to know what Danny was reading in the public library.

Reuven's walk to Danny's house at the beginning of Chapter 18 allows him time to reflect on the many events that have occurred since he was struck in the eye at the start of the novel. Because it is early spring, sycamore trees are budding and "green shoots of infant leaves" are appearing. Contrasted to this spring picture of rebirth are Reuven's memories of his numerous encounters with Reb Saunders. Whereas before Reuven only *noted* the bare walls and exposed light bulbs in Reb Saunders' synagogue, now he *evaluates* these features: "The stands were scarred, the walls needed paint, the naked light bulbs seemed ugly, their bare, black wires like the dead branches of a stunted tree." Here, the image of dead branches contrasts the newly budding sycamore branches mentioned earlier in the chapter. Outside, the world is alive with spring; inside Reb Saunders' house, the mood is one of death and decay. Even Reb Saunders himself personifies this decay. Reuven notes that Danny's father sits "stooped forward, bent, as though he were carrying something on his shoulders."

The climactic discussion between Reb Saunders, Danny, and Reuven is less dramatic than may be expected, for Reb Saunders is resigned to his son's decision to seek a Ph.D. in psychology. Symbolically, as though giving himself spiritual support, Reb Saunders rubs his fingers over the spine of his Talmud: "[H]is fingers caressed the Hebrew title of the tractate that was stamped into the spine of the binding." As expected, he talks to Danny through Reuven.

In his explanation of why he raised Danny in silence, Reb Saunders finally defines his own world philosophy. People are born with only a small amount of goodness in them; this goodness is comparable to a person's soul. However, when Danny was very young, he was a "mind in a body without a soul." That is, Danny intellectualized everything rather than emotionally feeling the pain and suffering of others. Danny's head ruled his heart, which Reb Saunders abhorred. Speaking of such a mind as Danny's, which is similar to Reb Saunders' own brother's, the Reb says, "It could not understand pain, it was indifferent to and impatient with suffering." Determined not to let Danny grow up without an understanding of the world's pain, Reb Saunders refused to talk to his son, except about religion. In this way, Danny would suffer and thereby learn of other people's suffering. Silence, not language, is the great teacher, for words are "cruel, words play tricks, they distort what is in the heart, they conceal the heart, the heart speaks through silence."

Reb Saunders is resigned to the fact that Danny will live in the secular world because he now knows that Danny has a soul and not only a mind. Danny was raised in silence precisely for this reason, to give him a soul, to enable him to help people who suffer. The Reb says of his son, "I have no more fear now. All his life he will be a tzaddik. He will be a tzaddik for the world." Danny will reconcile his religious upbringing with his living in a secular world. Symbolically, Reb Saunders can now speak his son's name because he knows that Danny hears suffering in his heart rather than only intellectualizing it in his mind.

In the novel's last scene, in which Reuven and Danny briefly discuss their futures, Danny's having shaved off his beard and cut off his earlocks symbolize his entering a new, more secular world. To Mr. Malter's question of whether or not Danny will raise his own son in silence, Danny answers ambiguously: He will raise his son in silence if he "can't find another way." His answer emphasizes the fact that Danny is not making a complete break with Hasidism; he will continue to observe Hasidic teachings and beliefs. However, he is also open to the possibility of change, which the phrase "another way" suggests. Ultimately, then, Danny rejects the "trapped" mind of his father and spiritual mentor, Reb Saunders.

- **kiddush**   a ceremonial blessing.
- **schnapps**   a liquor with high alcoholic content.
- **tractate**   a treatise or dissertation.
- **Passover**   a Jewish holiday in the spring, celebrating the Jews' exodus from slavery to freedom in ancient Egypt.

CHARACTER ANALYSES

DANNY SAUNDERS

The conflict between Danny's desire for secular knowledge and his desire to follow his Jewish faith is one of the main themes in *The Chosen*. Danny is being groomed to succeed his father, Reb Saunders, as the leader, or tzaddik, of a group of Hasidic Jews. But Danny does not want to follow this path—an intellectual person with a brilliant mind, he wants to be a psychologist. This conflict causes him much sadness; he is described throughout the novel as "weary" and "like a bird in pain," and he refers to himself as "trapped." As a Hasidic Jew, he is forced to live in a world that inhibits him.

Because Danny finds studying only the sacred text of the Talmud, a principal activity of ultra-Orthodox Jewish males, too limiting, he secretly goes to a public library to read classical Western literature, as well as books about psychology and Jewish history, which is forbidden by the tenets of his religious sect. However, by the end of the novel, he is able to find a balance between the religious and secular worlds, which is why his father can release him from his obligation to become a rabbi and accept his becoming a psychologist.

Danny remains dedicated to an Orthodox way of life, although not necessarily a Hasidic one, which seems to content his father. Instead of being a tzaddik for his father's congregation, he will be "a tzaddik for the world"—as his father acknowledges, "the world needs a tzaddik."

REB SAUNDERS

Reb Saunders personifies the Hasidic rebbe (from "rabbi," or teacher) and personifies strict, traditional, Orthodox Judaism. He led his followers out of Russia to the United States to escape physical persecution by the secular authorities. The Reb and his disciples devote themselves to a life similar to that led by their ancestors in the eighteenth century, including strict, ultra-Orthodox religious rules and customs and a unique style of dress, including long black coats, round fur hats, and Jewish prayer shawls underneath their clothes. They remain largely isolated from the outside, secular world, believing that their religious practices are vastly more important than world knowledge and, thus, must be protected from secular threats. Reb Saunders and his congregation expect that Danny, his son, will follow the Hasidic tradition and assume his father's position.

The Reb acknowledges that Danny is brilliant and that it would be fruitless to try to rein in his abilities. This decision does not come without a price, however. By the last scene in the novel, the Reb is described as a weakened, tired man whose "dark eyes brooded and burned with suffering." Even though he accepts that Danny will not follow in his footsteps as leader of his people, the "loss" of his son takes a great toll on him. Just as Danny finds it difficult to reconcile his secular interests with his religious obligations, Reb Saunders has difficulty reconciling his responsibility as a tzaddik to his people with his role as a father. He tells Danny, "A wiser father . . . may have done differently. I am not . . . wise." He does remain the unquestioned leader of his congregation, however. For example, when he authoritatively announces Danny's decision not to become the next tzaddik, "no one dared to challenge" the decision.

REUVEN MALTER

Like Danny, Reuven, the narrator of *The Chosen*, is an Orthodox Jew. But unlike Danny, Reuven can enter the secular world while still retaining his Jewish identity. Interestingly, though, Reuven wants to become a rabbi, while Danny, who is expected to become a rabbi, does not. Perhaps having the freedom to choose what he wants to be in life makes it easier for Reuven to opt for the religious path. Because his father never demands that Reuven become a rabbi, the position remains a possibility rather than an already determined demand. Had Mr. Malter commanded Reuven to be ordained a rabbi, perhaps Reuven would have rejected his father's wish, much like Danny seems to do.

Reuven experiences a great deal of growth throughout the novel. At the beginning of the story, his left eye is injured during a softball game. Although his physical sight is later restored, we see that, metaphorically, he *is* "blind." At first, he sees Danny only as a Hasidic Jew, not as an individual with thoughts and desires of his own. He looks at Danny and thinks, "Suddenly I had the feeling that everything around me was out of focus." But under the guidance of his father, Mr. Malter, Reuven eventually learns to look beneath the surface of his everyday experiences and perceptions. Not only does he open his mind to Danny, but he also is able to see Reb Saunders as much more than a fanatical, cold-hearted dictator.

DAVID MALTER

In contrast to Reb Saunders, David Malter recognizes the importance of secular knowledge. Thus Mr. Malter can allow his son, Reuven, to select a profession in the secular world and still be confident that Reuven will practice Orthodox Judaism (although Reuven ultimately decides to become a rabbi). As a Modern Orthodox Jew, Mr. Malter finds a balance between practicing his faith and remaining active in the world at large.

A basic difference between Mr. Malter and Reb Saunders is that Mr. Malter wants to do something in *this* world to help the survivors of the Nazi mass murder of Jews; thus he works hard in the Zionist movement toward the creation of a Jewish homeland in Palestine. In contrast, Reb Saunders can only wail at the slaughter of the Jews and say that it must have been the will of God. This contrast between the two men shows that while Reb Saunders is rooted in the spiritual world, which tells him that God determines men's fates, Mr. Malter is more practical, scientific, and Western-oriented. He uses logical reasoning to interpret issues, questioning data and discussing different points of view, whereas Reb Saunders explodes with feeling and passion on issues, sometimes at the expense of logic. However, Mr. Malter certainly is not without feelings. For example, we can see in his relationship with his son that he is a kind and loving man.

CRITICAL ESSAYS

CONFLICTING CULTURES IN THE NOVEL

The predicament of Danny Saunders lies at the core of Potok's *The Chosen*: Should Danny remain in the very ethnic world of the ultra-Orthodox Hasidic Jews, or should he reach out to join mainstream American culture? In this regard, Danny's predicament symbolizes the concern of many Jews in the United States.

The background against which Danny must make his decision about how much to assimilate into popular culture is the changing political and cultural situation of Jews in the late eighteenth and early nineteenth centuries. For hundreds of years, Jews were excluded physically and intellectually from the predominantly Christian civilization. They lived in their own world. As long as their communities, called ghettos, paid taxes and acted in a passive, almost subservient manner, they were allowed to exist peaceably. Their schools taught mostly traditional Jewish texts, with little instruction in secular affairs.

The French Revolution of 1789 had a great impact on Jews and their communities. To a certain extent, more and more Jews were prompted to enter mainstream society. However, a new dilemma arose for them—the same kind of dilemma that Danny Saunders faces in *The Chosen*: How much of the secular culture can a Jew absorb without completely giving up religion?

This question seems to be answered better by Reuven than by Danny. Reuven has integrated his Modern Orthodox faith and American culture. But Danny is not allowed to go to movies and must wear the same kind of clothing that his ancestors did. At the end of the novel, however, Danny decides to cut off his earlocks, wear modern clothes, and yet still observe the Jewish commandments in an Orthodox fashion as he always has done.

Interestingly, Reb Saunders, the most dogmatic character in the novel, seems to change as well. He realizes that he cannot keep Danny, with his brilliant mind, sequestered from the modern world. As he says, "This is America. This is not Europe. It is an open world here. . . . All his life he will be a tzaddik. He will be a tzaddik for the world. And the world needs a tzaddik."

When Reb Saunders asks Danny if he will shave off his beard and cut his earlocks when he goes away to college, Danny nods his head "yes." And when the Reb then asks him if he will continue to observe Hasidic customs, Danny again nods. Because Danny vows to remain faithful to Hasidic customs, Reb Saunders seems more accepting of his son's decision than if Danny had completely broken from his father's religion. However, the Reb is still saddened at the "loss" of his son. He knows that the secular world calls to Danny and that he cannot force his son to accept the religious position.

Danny's studying at Columbia University and yet pledging to remain an observant Jew indicates that he has grown closer to the culturally balanced world of Reuven Malter. Reuven adroitly moves between a secular culture, symbolized throughout the novel by his interest in world events, and a religious one, best emphasized by his ability to discuss Talmudic law both in class and with Reb Saunders. Although the novel ends without the reader having seen Danny completely immersed in his studies at Columbia, we expect that Danny will thrive in the highly intellectual university environment while, at the same time, respecting his father's wishes—perhaps unspoken but of great importance—that he remain devoted to the Hasidic religion in which he was raised.

THE FILM VERSION OF THE NOVEL

Readers of *The Chosen* can benefit from seeing the film version of the novel. The film gives a visually detailed view of the life of Hasidic Jews, including how they dress and perform religious rituals. Although both the novel and the film version concentrate on many of the same themes, the film version differs most from the novel in terms of the significance of Reuven's hospital stay following the accident during the softball game, and the treatment of women.

The movie opens, as does the novel, with a softball game. The viewer immediately gets an insight into Hasidim (the people of the sect of Hasidism), represented by Danny Saunders' team, which has come to play the team of Reuven Malter, a Modern Orthodox Jew. The Hasidim wear long black coats, wide-brimmed hats, and prayer shawls, the fringes of which hang out of their clothes at the waists. This style of dress has remained the same since the sect was founded in eighteenth-century Europe.

However old-fashioned and backward-looking the Hasidim may appear to outsiders, they know how to play softball, and they're very good at it, too. In fact, the star player for the Hasidic team, Danny Saunders, is so good that he hits the ball at the pitcher (Reuven) with enough force to smash Reuven's glasses and send him to the hospital. Reuven and Danny might not have met had it not been for the softball game, by Reuven's own admission.

The film differs from the book in that the six-day hospital stay described in the novel is reduced to one brief hospital scene in the film. The conversations between Danny and Reuven, Reuven and his father, and the three of them that take place over six days in the book are spread throughout the movie.

This restructuring of the film sharpens the focus of the relationship between Danny and Reuven. Many of their interactions take place in each other's homes, where the film audience is not distracted by the peripheral conversations and activities that take place in the novel. A more intimate relationship between Danny and Reuven becomes possible.

For example, in the film, Danny tells Reuven about his photographic memory at the latter's home. Reuven is skeptical, so he hands a newspaper to Danny. The look on his face says, in effect, "Show me, Danny." Danny does, and Reuven is astonished. In the novel, Reuven simply accepts at face value Danny's assertion that he has a photographic memory; he requires no proof.

Probably the most important difference between the novel and the movie version is that the movie allows us to see Danny and Reuven as adolescent teenagers interested in having a social life. In the novel, the two boys have endless discussions about religion and philosophy, but they rarely talk about the opposite sex. Danny's lack of interest in anything romantic can be explained by Hasidic marriage customs, in which boys and girls are matched early in life and have no choice about whom they marry.

Of course, in the novel, female characters receive less treatment than do male characters. Hasidic Judaism is a patriarchal society wherein women's primary roles are to bear and raise children (admittedly very important roles) and tend to the daily upkeep of the home. The only time women appear in the novel are brief scenes in which Danny's mother and sister are present. Reuven briefly mentions being interested in Danny's sister, but we don't even learn her name. Reuven's deceased mother is only casually mentioned, as is Reuven and Mr. Malter's Russian housekeeper, Manya, who, when she first greets Reuven on his arrival home from the hospital, "began to babble in Ukrainian." Potok's characterization of Manya is less than flattering.

The film version of *The Chosen* treats romantic interests differently. For example, in one scene, everyone is celebrating the end of World War II. Amid the merry-making, girls are kissing boys, including one girl who kisses Danny. He resists the kiss and afterward wipes it off his lips with his sleeve. Hasidic men are allowed to kiss only their wives.

But Reuven, a Modern Orthodox Jew, demonstrates an interest in the opposite sex. Unlike Danny, he approaches females with an intention to start a relationship. Whereas in the novel Reuven notices Danny's sister but we don't know her name, in the movie we discover that her name is Sheindl (**Shane** dull). In one scene in the film, Sheindl sits on a couch in her family's living room, reading. Reuven tries to see the title of the book and moves toward her on the couch. She moves away, and the two play a rather coy cat-and-mouse game until Sheindl's mother calls for her to help in the kitchen.

We also see Reuven at a boy-girl party at his home. He takes a girl's hand, leads her out into the hallway, and kisses her.

And yet another scene details a Hasidic wedding. By custom, a partition separates the males from the females, and they do not dance together. Reuven dares to go past the partition, catches Sheindl's eye, and smiles at her. She returns the smile. Alarmed at this, Mrs. Saunders beckons Danny to tell Reuven about the Hasidic marriage custom.

REVIEW QUESTIONS AND ESSAY TOPICS

(1) Compare the Modern Orthodox world of Reuven Malter and the Hasidic world of Danny Saunders. Cite examples from the novel that support how these two worlds differ from one another.

(2) Why does Potok begin the novel with Danny's and Reuven's softball teams playing each other?

(3) What is the significance of Reuven's eye being damaged by Danny during the softball game?

(4) Does Potok seem to support Reb Saunders' Hasidic viewpoints or Mr. Malter's less strictly religious beliefs? Or is Potok able to balance both viewpoints and not choose one over the other?

(5) Write an essay in which you compare Reuven and his father's relationship with Danny and his father's. Discuss the differences in how each set of father and son express their feelings for each other.

(6) Although *The Chosen* concerns Danny's coming of age in terms of his finding a personal identity separate from his father and his father's religion, Danny's struggle has been described as universal in that he represents other young adults. What examples in the novel support the view that Danny represents any person his age discovering a personal identity?

(7) What is Reuven's greatest challenge at the end of the novel? Does his future seem brighter or bleaker than Danny's?

(8) Part of Danny's dilemma involves wanting to be a psychologist and yet feeling that he must succeed his father as leader of their Hasidic sect. How does he work through this conflict, or does he?

(9) Write an essay in which you discuss why Reb Saunders raises Danny in silence. Do the ill health of Danny's mother and her generally neutral presence play a role in the Reb's attitude toward his son? Support your answer with examples from the novel.

(10) Compare Reb Saunders' and Mr. Malter's reactions to the murder of 6 million Jews in Europe during World War II. How does each man's reaction characterize his philosophy of life? Does Potok agree with one view more than with the other, or does he create a balanced interpretation between them?

SELECTED BIBLIOGRAPHY

BOOKS ABOUT JUDAISM

BULKA, REUVEN. *Dimensions of Orthodox Judaism*. New York: Ktav, 1983.

BAMBERGER, BERNARD. *The Story of Judaism*. New York: Schocken Books, 1971.

BERSHTAL, SARA, and ALLEN GRAUBARD. *Saving Remnants: Feeling Jewish in America*. New York: Free Press, 1992.

BIRNBAUM, PHILIP. *Encyclopedia of Jewish Concepts*. New York: Hebrew Publishing Co., 1988.

DANZGER, HERBERT. *Returning to Tradition*. New Haven, Connecticut: Yale University Press, 1989.

EMBER, MELVIN, and DAVID LEVINSON. *American Immigrant Cultures: Builders of a Nation*. New York: Simon and Schuster, 1997.

GUTTMAN, ALLEN. *The Jewish Writer in America: Assimilation and the Crisis of Identity*. New York: Oxford University Press, 1971.

HARRIS, LIS. *Holy Days: The World of a Hasidic Family.* New York: Collier Books, 1985.

HEILMAN, SAMUEL. *Cosmopolitans and Parochials: Modern Orthodox Jews in America.* Chicago: University of Chicago Press, 1989.

POLL, SOLOMON. *The Hasidic Community of Williamsburg.* New York: Schocken Books, 1969.

SORIN, GERALD. *A Time for Building: The Third Migration, 1880-1920.* Baltimore: Johns Hopkins University Press, 1992.

WIGODER, GEOFFREY, ed. *American Jewish Memoirs.* Jerusalem: Institute of Contemporary Judaism, 1980.

CRITICAL WORKS ABOUT POTOK

ABRAMSON, EDWARD. *Chaim Potok.* Boston: Twayne Publishers, 1986.

BLUEFARB, SAM. "The Head, the Heart, and the Conflict of Generations in Chaim Potok's *The Chosen.*" *College Language Association Journal,* June 1971.

GITTELSON, NATALIE. "American Jews Re-Discover Orthodoxy." *The New York Times Magazine,* September 30, 1984.

HEILMAN, SAMUEL, "Inner and Outer Identities: Social Ambivalence Among Orthodox Jews." *Jewish Social Studies,* Summer 1977.

POTOK, CHAIM. "Culture Confrontation in Urban America: A Writer's Beginning." In *Literature and the Urban Experience: Essays on the City and Literature.* Eds. A. C. Watts and M. C. Jaye. New Brunswick, New Jersey: Rutgers University Press, 1981.

SHAPIRO, KARL. "The Necessary People." *The Washington Post*, April 23, 1967.

WALDEN, DANIEL. *The World of Chaim Potok*. Studies in American Jewish Literature. Vol. 4. Albany, New York: SUNY Press, 1985.

WATTS, A. C. and M. C. JAYE. *Literature and the Urban Experience: Essays on the City and Literature*. New Brunswick, New Jersey: Rutgers University Press, 1981.

CPSIA information can be obtained at www.ICGtesting.com
Printed in the USA
BVOW02s1759090414

350179BV00001B/35/P